ARISTOPHANES' CLOUDS

ARISTOPHANES' CLOUDS

**Translated
With Introduction
and Notes**

Jeffrey Henderson
Boston University

Focus Classical Library
Focus Information Group, Inc.
PO Box 369
Newburyport MA 01950

THE FOCUS CLASSICAL LIBRARY

Series Editors • James Clauss and Stephen Esposito

Aristophanes: Acharnians • Jeffrey Henderson
Aristophanes: The Birds • Jeffrey Henderson
Aristophanes: Clouds • Jeffrey Henderson
Aristophanes: Frogs • Henderson
Aristophanes: Lysistrata • Jeffrey Henderson
Aristophanes: Three Comedies: Acharnians, Lysistrata, Clouds • Jeffrey Henderson
Euripides: The Bacchae • Stephen Esposito
Euripides: Four Plays: Medea, Hippolytus, Heracles, Bacchae • Stephen Esposito, ed.
Euripides: Hecuba • Robin Mitchell-Boyask
Euripides: Heracles • Michael R. Halleran
Euripides: Hippolytus • Michael R. Halleran
Euripides: Medea • Anthony Podlecki
Euripides: The Trojan Women • Diskin Clay
Golden Verses: Poetry of the Augustan Age • Paul T. Alessi
Golden Prose in the Age of Augustus • Paul T. Alessi
Hesiod: Theogony • Richard Caldwell
Hesiod: Theogony & Works and Days • Stephanie Nelson
The Homeric Hymns • Susan Shelmerdine
Ovid: Metamorphoses • Z. Philip Ambrose
Plautus: Captivi, Amphitryon, Casina, Pseudolus • David Christenson
Roman Comedy: Five Plays by Plautus and Terence • David Christenson
Roman Lives • Brian K. Harvey
Sophocles: Antigone • Ruby Blondell
Sophocles: Electra • Hanna M. Roisman
Sophocles: King Oidipous • Ruby Blondell
Sophocles: Oidipous at Colonus • Ruby Blondell
Sophocles: Philoktetes • Seth Schein
Sophocles: The Theban Plays • Ruby Blondell
Terence: Brothers (Adelphoe) • Charles Mercier
Vergil: The Aeneid • Richard Caldwell

Copyright © 1992 by Jeffrey Henderson

ISBN 10: 0-941051-24-2
ISBN 13: 978-0-941051-24-8

This book is published by Focus Publishing / R. Pullins Company, PO Box 369, Newburyport MA 01950. All rights are reserved. No part of this publication may be produced, stored in a retrieval system, produced on stage or otherwise performed, transmitted by any means, electronic, mechanical, by photocopying, recording, or by any other media or means without the prior written permission of the publisher.

19 18 17 16 15 14 13 12 11 10 9

1209TS

For my brothers,
Bruce and David

Contents

Preface

Clouds, first performed in 423 BC, is a comedy about the revolutionary social, intellectual and educational changes that characterized the Athenian enlightenment of the late fifth century and that would profoundly shape the subsequent course of Western history. At its center is the philosopher, Socrates, who is portrayed as the arch-sophist, running an educational cult (the 'Thinkery') in which young men could pay to learn the latest scientific lore and rhetorical skills in order to achieve fame, power and wealth. In the Thinkery are two Arguments: the Better, an old gentleman who represents traditional customs, beliefs and virtues, and the Worse, a young dandy who advocates the techniques of unscrupulous self-promotion and the desirability of selfish hedonism. Drawn to the Thinkery is the forgetful old rustic Strepsiades, who has run up huge debts as a result of his son Pheidippides' passion for horses and who wants to learn how to evade them. Unable to learn the new techniques himself, Strepsiades forces Pheidippides to enroll in the Thinkery. Strepsiades' wish comes true in that Pheidippides emerges from the Thinkery as a skilled sophist, easily able to evade debts by dishonest arguments. At the same time, however, he has become so arrogant and amoral that he beats up Strepsiades and convinces him that it is just to do so. But when Pheidippides proposes to beat up his mother as well, Strepsiades realizes what a terrible mistake he has made and takes vengeance on Socrates by burning the Thinkery to the ground. Above the action float the Chorus of Clouds: in their protean whimsicality they seem appropriate goddesses for Socrates, but they gradually reveal themselves to be a wishing mirror for people in love with evil, luring them to a well deserved punishment.

Clouds is both a hilarious comedy of generational conflict and a profound exploration of some of the most fundamental conflicts in Western culture: belief versus reason, nature versus culture, religion versus science, the community versus the individual. It also contains a priceless portrait of one of the most gifted and influential men in history, a man otherwise known only from the adulatory writings of such pupils as Plato and Xenophon. Aristophanes' portrait, written from the perspective of a popular humorist of traditional bent, is often in fascinating disagreement with that of the philosophers, and it proved trenchant enough that Plato called it a significant factor in Socrates' condemnation twenty-four years later.

Today *Clouds* is just as entertaining as theater, and just as relevant as a view of the best and worst of Western civilization, as it was over two millennia ago. In its mirror modern people can catch a glimpse of where we came from, where our best ideals have aimed us, and how far we have come (or not come) thus far.

This is a translation of *Clouds* into contemporary American verse, designed for both readers and performers, and presupposing no knowledge of classical Greece or classical Greek theater. I render the Greek text line by line so as to give a sense of its original scope and pace, using for the dialogue and songs verse-forms that are familiar to modern audiences. Where the original text refers to people, places, things and events whose significance modern audiences cannot reasonably be expected to know or to infer from the text, and which are inessential to its main themes, I have tried to find easily comprehensible alternatives that preserve the import of the original. What may be unfamiliar in the text is discussed in footnotes.

The conventions of Aristophanic comedy include the frank portrayal and discussion of religion, politics and sex (including nudity and obscenity). I have reproduced this feature as accurately as possible within my general guideline of easy intelligibility. To do otherwise would be to falsify the play. These three areas are of fundamental importance to any society; one of Aristophanes' chief aims was to make humor of them while at the same time encouraging his audience to think about them in ways discouraged, or even forbidden, outside the comic theater. The issue of freedom of speech and thought (especially religious and moral thought) is especially relevant to *Clouds*. For those made uncomfortable by such provocative theater, *Clouds* provides an opportunity to ask themselves why.

The Introduction contains sections on Aristophanes and the genre of Attic Old Comedy which his plays represent; on *Clouds* and the Athenian enlightenment; on conventions of ancient production, with suggestions for modern performers; and suggestions for further reading. Like the translation and notes, the Introduction requires no previous expertise, and so is suitable for readers and students making their first acquaintance with Aristophanes.

The translation is based on the Greek text by Sir Kenneth Dover (Oxford 1968).

JJH
Boston
August 1992

INTRODUCTION

Aristophanes and Old Comedy

The period of Old Comedy at Athens began in 486 BC, when comedy first became part of the festival of the Greater Dionysia, and by convention ended in 388 BC, when Aristophanes produced his last play. During this period some 600 comedies were produced. We know the names of some fifty comic poets and the titles of some 300 plays. We have eleven complete plays by Aristophanes, the first one dating from 425, and several thousand fragments of other plays by Aristophanes and other poets, most of them only a line or so long and very few from plays written before 440.

The principal occasion for the production of comedies were the Greater Dionysia, held in March or April, and (from 440) the Lenaea, held in January or February. These were national festivals honoring the wine-god Dionysus (whose cult from very early times had included mimetic features), and the theatrical productions were competitions in which poets, dancers, actors, producers and musicians competed for prizes that were awarded by judges at the close of the festival. The Greater Dionysia was held in the Theater of Dionysus on the south slope of the Acropolis and accommodated some 17,000 spectators, who included both Athenian and foreign visitors. The Lenaea, which only Athenians attended, was held elsewhere in the city (we do not know where). By the fourth century the Lenaea was held in the Theater of Dionysus also, but it is unclear when the relocation occurred.

At these festivals comedy shared the theater with tragedy and satyr-drama, which had been produced at the Greater Dionysia since the sixth century. The first contest in tragedy is dated to 534 (the poet Thespis was victorious), but it is not certain that this contest was held at the Greater Dionysia, and in any case this festival seems to have experienced major changes after the overthrow of the tyranny and the establishment of democracy, that is, after 508. Tragedy dramatized stories from heroic myth, emphasizing dire personal and social events that had befallen hero(in)es and their families in the distant past and mostly in places other than Athens. By convention, the poetry and music of tragedy were highly stylized and archaic. Satyr-drama, which was composed by the same poets who wrote tragedy, was the same, except that the heroic stories were treated in a humorous fashion and the chorus was composed of satyrs: mischievous followers of Dionysus who were part human and part animal.

Comedy, by contrast, had different conventions of performance (see on page 14, below) and was less restricted by conventions of language, music and subject. That is probably why the composers and performers of tragedy and satyr-drama were never the same ones who composed and performed comedy. The language of comedy was basically colloquial, though it often parodies the conventions of other (particularly tragic) poetry, and was free to include indecent, even obscene material. The music and dancing, too, tended to reflect popular styles. The favorite subjects of comedy were free-form mythological burlesque; domestic situations featuring everyday character types; and political satire portraying people and events of current interest in the public life of the Athenians. Our eleven surviving comedies all fall into this last category. Mythological and domestic comedy continued to flourish after the Old Comic period, but political comedy seems to have died out: a casualty of social and political changes following the Athenians' loss of the Peloponnesian War, and with it their empire, in 404. To understand the significance of political comedy, we must look first at the political system of which it was an organic feature: the phase of radical democracy inaugurated by the reforms of Ephialtes in 462/1 and lasting until the end of the century.

Democracy means 'rule of the demos' (sovereign people). In fifth-century Athens democracy was radical in that the sovereignty of the demos was more absolute than in any other society before or since. The demos consisted of all citizen males at least eighteen years of age. All decisions affecting the governance and welfare of the state were made by the direct and unappealable vote of the demos. The state was managed by members of the demos at least thirty years of age who were chosen by lot from a list of eligible citizens and who held office in periods ranging from one day to one year. The only exceptions were military commanders, who were elected to one-year terms, and holders of certain ancient priesthoods, who inherited their positions. The demos determined by vote whether or not anyone holding any public position was qualified to do his job, and after completion of his term, whether he had done it satisfactorily. All military commanders, and most holders of powerful allotted offices came from the wealthy classes but their success depended on the good will of the demos as a whole.

One of the most important allotted offices was that of choregus (sponsor of a chorus). Choregoi were allotted from a list of men wealthy enough to hold this office, for they had to recruit and pay for the training, costuming and room and board of the chorus that would perform at one of the festivals. In the case of a comic chorus this involved 24 dancers and the musicians who would accompany them. Being choregus gave a man an opportunity to display his wealth and refinement for the benefit of the demos as a whole and to win a prize that would confer prestige on himself and his dancers. Some wealthy men therefore volunteered to be choregus instead of waiting for their names to be drawn. On the other hand, a man who put on a cheap or otherwise unsatisfactory chorus could expect to suffer a significant loss of public prestige.

All other expenses, including stipends for the poet and his actors and for prizes, were undertaken by vote of the demos and paid for from public funds. A poet got a place in the festival by submitting a draft some six months in advance to the office-holder in charge of the festival. Ancient sources say that at least the choral parts of the proposed play had to be submitted. How much more was submitted we do not know. But revision up to the day of the performance was certainly possible, since many allusions in comedy refer to events occurring very shortly before the festival: most notably the death of Sophocles shortly before the performance of *Frogs* in 405.

If he got on the program, the poet would be given his stipend and assigned his actors. He and the choregus would then set about getting the performance ready for the big day, the poet acting as music master, choreographer and director, the choregus rounding up and paying the expenses of the best dancers he could find. While tragic poets produced three tragedies and a satyr-drama, comic poets produced only one comedy.

Thus comedy, as a theatrical spectacle, was an organic feature of Athenian democracy. But its poetic, musical and mimetic traditions were much older, deriving from forms of entertainment developed by cultivated members of the aristocratic families that had governed Attica before the democracy. One such form was the komos (band of revellers), which gave comedy (komoidia: 'song of the komos') its name. A komos was made up of some solidary group (a military, religious or family group, for example), often in disguise, which entertained onlookers on many kinds of festive and religious occasions.

Part of the entertainment was abuse and criticism of individuals or groups standing outside the solidarity of the komos. The victims might be among the onlookers or they might be members of a rival komos. The komos sang and danced as a group, and its leader (who was no doubt also the poet) could speak by himself to his komos, to the onlookers or to a rival komos-leader. No doubt at a very early stage komos was a competitive entertainment by which a given group could, in artistic ways, make those claims and criticisms against rival groups which at other times they might make in more overtly political ways.

Aside from its value as entertainment, the tradition of the komos was useful in allowing the expression of personal and political hostilities which would otherwise have been difficult to express safely: the misbehavior of powerful individuals, disruptive but unactionable gossip, the shortcomings of citizens in groups or as a whole. In this capacity komos served as a social safety valve, allowing a relatively harmless airing of tensions before they could become dangerous, and also as a means of social communication and social control, upholding generally held norms and calling attention to derelictions.

But in addition to its critical and satiric aspects, komos (like all festive activities) had an idealistic side, envisaging the community as it would be if everyone agreed on norms and lived up to them, and a utopian side as well, imagining how wonderful life would be if reality were as human beings would like it to be. In this capacity komos provided a welcome relief from the cares and burdens of everyday life.

Old Comedies were theatrical versions of komos: the band of dancers with their leader was now a comic chorus involved in a story enacted by actors on a stage. The chorus still resembled a komos in two ways. As performers, it competed against rival choruses, and in its dramatic identity it initially represented a distinct group or groups: in *Clouds*, for example, it initially represents the guiding spirits of Socrates' Thinkery. The comic chorus differs from a komos in that at a certain point in the play it drops its dramatic identity and thereafter represents the celebrating community as a whole. At this point, its leader steps forward, on behalf of the poet, to advise and admonish the spectators, and his chorus might sing abusive songs about particular individuals in the audience.

The actors in the stage-area had been amalgamated with the chorus during the sixth century. Their characteristic costumes (page 14, below) and antics were depicted in vase-paintings of that period in many parts of Greece, suggesting a much older tradition of comic mimesis. As early as the Homeric period (eighth and seventh centuries) we find mythological burlesque and such proto-comedy as the Thersites episode in the second book of the *Iliad*. In this period, too, the iambic poets flourished. Named for the characteristic rhythm of their verses, which also became the characteristic rhythm of actors in Athenian drama, the iambic poets specialized in self-revelation, popular story-telling, earthy gossip, and personal enmities, often creating fictitious first-person identities and perhaps also using masks and disguise. They were credited with pioneering poetic styles of invective, obscenity and colloquialism.

The characters on the Old Comic stage preserved many of these traditions, but like the chorus they were an adaptation to the democratic festivals, most notably in political comedy. In Aristophanes's plays, the world depicted by the plot and the characters on stage was the world of the spectators in their civic roles: as heads of families and participants in governing the state. We see the demos in its various capacities; the competitors for public influence; the men who hold or seek offices; the social, intellectual and artistic celebrities. We hear formal debate on current issues, including its characteristic invective. We get a decision, complete with winners and losers, and we see the outcome. This depiction of public life was designed both to arouse laughter and to encourage reflection about people and events in ways not possible in other public contexts. Thus it was at once a distorted and an accurate depiction of public life, like a modern political cartoon.

Aristophanic comedies typically depict Athens in the grip of a terrible and intractable problem (e.g. the war, bad political leaders, an unjust jury-system, dangerous artistic or intellectual trends) which is solved in a fantastic but essentially plausible way, often by a comic hero. The characters of these heroic plays fall into two main categories, sympathetic and unsympathetic. The sympathetic ones (the hero and his/her supporters), are fictitious creations embodying ideal civic types or representing ordinary Athenians. The unsympathetic ones embody disapproved civic behavior and usually represent specific leaders or categories of leaders. The sympathetic characters advocate positions held by political or social minorities and are therefore 'outsiders'. But they are shown winning out against the unsympathetic ones, who represent the current status quo. Characters or chorus-members representing the demos as a whole are portrayed as initially sceptical or hostile to the sympathetic character(s), but in the end they are persuaded; those responsible for the problem are disgraced or expelled, and Athens is recalled to a sense of her true (traditional) ideals and is thus renewed. In the (thoroughly democratic) comic view, the people are never at fault for their problems, but are merely good people who have been deceived by bad leaders. Thus the comic poets tried to persuade the actual demos (the spectators) to change its mind about issues that had been decided but might be changed, or (as in *Clouds*) to discard dangerous novelties. Aristophanes at least once succeeded: after the performance of *Frogs* he was awarded a crown by the city for the advice given by the chorus leader in that play and subsequently adopted by the demos.

In this way, the institution of Old Comedy performed functions essential to any democracy: public airing of minority views and criticism of those holding power. In this function, the Old Comic festivals were organized protest. But they were also an opportunity to articulate civic ideals: one identified the shortcomings of the status quo by holding it up against a vision of things as they ought to (or used to) be. The use of satire and criticism within a plot addressing itself to important issues of national scope was thus a democratic adaptation of such pre-democratic traditions as komos and iambic poetry. That the comic festivals were state-run and not privately organized is striking evidence of the openness and self-confidence of a full democracy: the demos was completely in charge, so it did not fear attacks on its celebrities or resent admonition by the poets. In particular, the Athenians were much less inclined than we are to treat their political leaders with fear and reverence: since the Athenian people were themselves the government, they tended to see their leaders more as advisors and competitors for public stature than august representatives of the state. In Socrates' case, the demos seems to have taken Aristophanes' criticisms to heart, however exaggerated they may have been: as Plato reported in his *Apology*, the *Clouds'* 'nonsensical' portrait of Socrates was a factor in the people's decision to condemn him to death.

The comic poets did not, however, enjoy complete license to say anything they pleased. Were that the case they could not have expected anyone to take what they had to say seriously. Following each festival there was an assembly in which anyone who had a legal complaint could come forward. Like any other public voices, comic poets had to avoid slander (malicious and unfounded abuse) and could not criticize the democratic constitution and the inherent rightness of the demos' rule. Nor could they speak ill of the (honorable) dead or compromise the integrity of the state religion. If the criticism and abuse we find in Old Comedy often seems outrageous by our standards, it is because we differ from the fifth-century Athenians in our definitions of outrageous, not because comic poets were held to no standards.

Aristophanes, for example, was twice sued by the politician Cleon, once for slandering the demos and its officers in front of visiting foreigners (in *Babylonians* of 426) and once for slandering Cleon himself (in *Knights* of 424). In the first instance the demos decided not to hear the case. In the second the poet and the politician settled out of court (Aristophanes subsequently boasted that he had not abided by the agreement). The demos could also enact new laws restricting comic freedoms. One of these was enacted in 440, when Athens went to war against her own ally Samos, another in 415, which forbade mention by name in comedy of any of the men who had recently been prosecuted for parodying the Eleusinian Mysteries of Demeter. Evidently the demos wanted these men to be officially forgotten and perhaps feared that mention of their names might pollute the festival. In addition, the demos did not want to take the chance that a comic poet might speak sympathetically of any of these men as comic poets often spoke for other underdogs; it is perhaps relevant that three of the men condemned seem to have been comic poets.

With these general characteristics of Old Comedy in mind, let us turn now to *Clouds* and its contribution to public entertainment and intellectual debate in the winter of 423 BC.

Clouds, Aristophanes and the Athenian Enlightenment

Clouds was originally produced at the Greater Dionysia in 423 BC, but placed third and last (Cratinus, whom Aristophanes had ridiculed as a washed-up old drunk, won the first prize). This defeat—Aristophanes' first after an initial string of victories—hurt and angered Aristophanes, for in the following year he called *Clouds* his best play and abused the spectators for rejecting it (in *Wasps* 1037-47). At some point he began to revise the play with a re-staging in mind, but for some reason he abandoned the revision before it was completed (internal evidence suggests a date between 419 and 416); perhaps he lost interest, and perhaps he was discouraged by friends or officials. Somehow the revised text got into circulation (probably by Aristophanes' friends or literary executors after his death). Although ancient editors had both the original festival version and the incomplete revision at their disposal, it is only the revised version that has survived.

Lack of evidence about the first version of *Clouds* makes it impossible to tell just how much Aristophanes altered in the process of his revision. Definitely new is the parabasis-speech (518-62) discussing the defeat of the original play and hoping for success with the new version. In other respects we must rely mainly on the testimony of an anonymous ancient scholar who wrote that 'the play has been revised everywhere; some parts have been removed, new sections woven in, and alterations made in arrangement and in the dialogue between characters. Some parts as they stand belong entirely to the revised version: thus the chorus' parabasis has been replaced, where Better Argument speaks to Worse [i.e. 889-948], and finally where Socrates' school is burned.

Clouds is a critical satire of the Athenian sophistic movement and its impact on ethics and education, an impact illustrated by the experience of a father and his son. In the play, the immortal philosopher Socrates (469-399), best known to posterity from the writings of his pupils Plato and Xenophon, typifies the sophistic movement, even though in reality he differed in important respects (as we will see) from other sophists. In *Clouds*, Socrates is portrayed as an impoverished guru who spends his contemplative hours suspended in a basket, the better to let his mind fly free. He is the master of a school called the Thinkery (Phrontisterion), where he closets himself with his young pupils, a flock of pale, unathletic eggheads who spend their time doing strange experiments and collecting useless knowledge. The Thinkery is supported by tuition fees and petty theft. Outside the Thinkery is a ceramic image of Vertigo (Dinos), whom the inhabitants revere instead of Zeus, along with other novel deities like Emptiness, Tongue, Air and Trickery. Prospective pupils must renounce Zeus and the traditional gods, vow to lead a life of asceticism and undergo a mystical initiation, as if they were joining a religious cult.

Drawn to this strange company is the old and wealthy country-villager, Strepsiades, who has run up mountainous debts as a result of his son Pheidippides' preoccupation with chariot-racing and the traditional aristocratic lifestyle that goes with it. He has heard that Socrates can teach anyone the ability to win any case, however unjust, and hopes that Socrates will teach his own son how to evade his debts. When Pheidippides refuses, Strepsiades enrolls himself. But he is unable to learn the new techniques, and finally bullies Pheidippides into reconsidering his refusal. In order to entice Pheidippides, Socrates stages a debate between two Arguments that he keeps in the Thinkery, the Better (a cranky old man who defends the traditional education) and the Worse (a suave young man who defends the new). Better Argument, who urges obedience and modesty, is utterly defeated by Worse Argument, who promises success and gratification. Better Argument deserts to the side of his opponent, so that Pheidippides must enroll in the Thinkery.

Meanwhile, Strepsiades confronts two of his creditors (one his own age, the other a friend of his son's) and refuses to repay them, (mis)using the lessons he had learned from Socrates. But it is clear that by doing this he has made himself a pariah in his village and will ultimately have to justify his behavior in court. Pheidippides then emerges from the Thinkery and assures Strepsiades that the debts will be no problem. Elated at the success of his son's education, Strepsiades invites him to a graduation feast. But things go terribly wrong. Pheidippides has renounced all the cultural bonds that had tied him to his father and has embraced the newest fashions; when Strepsiades

Greece and Environs

objects to Pheidippides' new attitudes and behavior, Pheidippides beats him up. Worse, he forces Strepsiades to agree that father-beating is justified. But when he offers to do the same for his own mother, Strepsiades finally sees the error of his ways and sets off to burn the Thinkery to the ground.

Among Aristophanes' plays *Clouds* is in many respects unusual, not least in its having no really sympathetic character. The role usually reserved for the sympathetic hero, who finds a way to right an unjust situation and to discredit those responsible, is occupied by an amusing but fundamentally unsympathetic character, Strepsiades. Instead of struggling against impossible odds to do what is right, Strepsiades struggles to do wrong; and instead of standing up against an evil authority (Socrates), Strepsiades joins forces with him in order to further his own nefarious scheme. In addition, he compels his normal and wholesome (if spoiled) son Pheidippides to submit to Socrates' teachings as well. As a result, both Strepsiades' family life and his standing in his village are destroyed, and so is Pheidippides' character. Strepsiades' sudden attack on Socrates' Thinkery at the very end of the play seems to be an essentially incoherent act of violence that in any case does nothing to undo the harm that Strepsiades has brought on himself and his family.

Clouds is also unusual in having no obvious moral center of gravity. The point of the play is to satirize and to expose the fraudulence of sophistic teaching by showing its ruinous effect on traditional values as they are exemplified by one family. But at the same time, by framing his satire in an anti-heroic plot in which victim and victimizer join forces and by caricaturing Better Argument, the only systematic defender of traditional values in the play, as vehemently as he does Worse Argument, Aristophanes seems to be emphasizing both the weakness of traditional values and their ready vulnerability to the corrupting influence of sophism. If Strepsiades, Pheidippides and Better Argument are typical representatives of traditional values, we are left with the impression that these values were pretty shallow to begin with. And when Better Argument is quite unable to make an adequate defence of his values when the chips are down and Pheidippides' soul is at stake, in what sense can we be expected to side with him anyway? Thus neither side in the great debate is given an admirable champion. When Socrates is burned out at play's end, it is not because his ideas have been formally discredited but because they have triumphed. Is the kind of incoherent and unprincipled violence that Strepsiades unleashes at the end the only possible response to the sophistic threat? This ambiguous outcome suggests that in *Clouds* Aristophanes created a true comedy of ideas that captured the perhaps ineluctable essence of a cultural dilemma that worried thinking Athenians and even in our own day has yet to be resolved. This dilemma can be stated rather simply: when a society suddenly generates serious intellectual challenges to the norms and beliefs that over long periods of time have given it cohesion and stability, how should people react?

This dilemma in its fifth-century form was precipitated by the influx of foreign intellectuals, scientists, technicians and teachers into Athens. Such men were attracted to Athens because she had become a prosperous imperial city as a result of her expansionist policies following the Persian invasions (which ended in 479) and a fertile ground for progressive thought, individual ambition and freedom of expression as a result of her adoption (in the 460s) of a fully democratic polity. The long political ascendancy of the aristocratic populist and intellectual Pericles (*c.* 490-429) did much to attract and encourage the avant garde of Greek intellectuals, who have come collectively to be known as 'sophists' (a word describing those possessing systematic technical, intellectual and social skills). Although this term covers a wide range of pursuits (natural and social sciences, philosophy and logic, linguistics and philology, musicology and literary criticism, theology and history, law and rhetoric) and a wide range of styles (from formal teaching and writing to mere hobbyism), a public stereotype of the typical sophist seems to have developed by Aristophanes' time. A sophist was a man, usually a foreigner, who possessed arcane knowledge and had untraditional, often counter-intuitive ideas, and who offered to teach these to anyone who could afford the high tuition fees.

A sophist's typical pupil was a well-to-do young man seeking an alternative to the traditional Athenian education, which combined athletic and military training with indoctrination in traditional values (such as honesty, modesty and deference to the gods and to the older generation) and in the music and poetry by which these were largely transmitted. Although some of these pupils were interested in the new education for its own sake, out of intellectual curiosity, many (perhaps the majority) had a more practical motivation. A young man aiming for power and public distinction in democratic Athens had to be a capable orator and debater, able to persuade the Assembly and to win in the law-courts. Many of the sophists claimed that they could teach these very skills and that the traditional education no longer could; as proof of their claim they could point to the meteoric success of a good many pupils, among them not only the great Pericles but also some of the most promising leaders of the next generation, like Alcibiades.

Aristophanes, reflecting the fear and resentment of the man in the street, portrays the sophists and their pupils in the most unfavorable light. Their intellectual concerns are useless and absurd. Worse, they are amoral, caring not about the justice of an argument but only how to win it, and atheistic, denying the existence of Zeus and the other traditional gods and substituting new deities of their own—deities reflecting their own selfish and dishonest ambitions. Because of their contempt for traditional community values, they teach the young to pursue wealth, power and pleasure at the expense of others and in whatever way they please, however shameless; to despise the laws; and to ignore the well-being of the state. As a result, many members of the younger generation have become either a reclusive rabble of pale eggheads or an amoral, disobedient cadre of greedy hedonists. As a result, the younger generation not only cannot be relied on to help safeguard the state, but they also invite the vengeance of the gods.

The plot required that someone represent the typical sophist, and Socrates was an obvious choice. Unlike most sophists, who were wealthy foreigners teaching in private for high fees and who were often away from Athens, Socrates was a native Athenian of average means who never left Athens and who spent his time in the market-place and the wrestling-schools, relentlessly questioning and arguing about anything and everything with whomever he could engage. He had a loyal following of restless and ambitious young men, including such celebrities as Alcibiades, who imitated him and who keenly enjoyed his ability to debunk the most formidable men of their fathers' generation. He was notoriously critical of unexamined beliefs (particularly religious ones) and of the (inevitably messy) processes of democratic polity. And he was charismatic: ugly in a compelling way, brilliant, courageous, visionary.

Most of Aristophanes' audience seem to have credited his por-trayal, to have felt that, despite its exaggerated and humorous fea-tures, the poet had voiced essentially their own views, since in 399 they condemned Socrates to death on charges of having corrupted the young and undermined the traditional religion. Socrates was lucky in having in his adoring pupils, Plato and Xenophon, two great defenders, so that he has been triumphantly acquitted by posterity of the charges that seemed justified in the eyes of his fellow-citizens. But if we set Plato and Xenophon to one side and try to imagine ourselves as ordinary contemporaries of Socrates, the Aristophanic caricature does not seem wholly unfair. Many of Socrates' followers did in fact do great harm to Athens, either by actively undermining or even (like Alcibiades) betraying the democracy, or (almost as bad) by refusing to participate in it. If Socrates seems not to have had an actual 'school' or to have taken money for tuition, he did keep company with the other sophists who did run schools and charge fees, and he was a frequent guest in the sumptuous houses of their pupils. And if Socra-tes did not pursue *sophia* in the same (largely technical) fashion as most sophists, he took a serious interest in the same pursuits, was in his own way the same kind of sceptic about traditional values and beliefs, and attracted the same young men to be his followers. Thus the later Platonic distinction between Socrates the *philosopher* (good) and the teachers of practical knowledge as *sophists* (bad) is a distinc-tion that few of Socrates' contemporaries would have cared to draw.

The contemporary conflict of generations and educational ideologies is well captured by the debate between the Arguments. Although it would have been easy simply to portray Better Argument (like Strepsiades' creditors) as being unfairly cheated of a rightful victory, Aristophanes instead chose to expose the strengths and weaknesses of both sides. Better Argument embodies the sort of attitudes that Strepsiades' generation held and hoped to pass on to their sons; these attitudes, he claims, made possible the astounding prosperity that Athens had achieved in his own time. But Better Argument cannot have appealed very strongly to the young men in the audience, with his ludicrously rosy version of the good old days and his tired harping on the virtues of obedience, modesty, deference, self-effacement and toil; his whole harangue amounts to a series of negatives. In addition, he seems obsessed with boys' genitals and emotionally repressed to an unhealthy degree. Worse Argument, by contrast, is a cheerful young hedonist who voices the positive injunctions that young men are always so eager to hear: find your own path, have fun, do as you like, be successful and wealthy, don't bother about your parents' wishes and advice. After all, he asks, who ever became successful by being modest? Even though Worse Argument's argument is specious at best, it is quite adequate to the task of refuting and silencing his opponent, whose only argument is blind obedience to tradition. Better Argument, Aristophanes seems to be suggesting, had better do better if young men like Pheidippides are to be recalled to the traditional education. That Aristophanes portrays Better Argument so lamely may reflect his personal experience. After all, Aristophanes was himself a member of the younger generation and therefore not immune to the effects of its enlightenment; no doubt he, like Pheidippides, had been torn between the pull of the old and the lure of the new.

Above the action of the characters in our drama float the ever-changing Clouds. At the beginning of the play they are invoked by Socrates as members of his new menagerie of scientific deities, embodying the airy fancies and daydreams of the new contemplative man and mirroring the protean structure of his ethical universe. The Clouds participate in luring Strepsiades into the Thinkery. But as the action develops, we gradually come to realize that the Clouds are in reality great powers aligned with Zeus and the traditional gods. Like the gods, they have the power to reward good and punish bad, and they lure evil-minded men like Strepsiades to disaster as an object lesson to all who would follow a similar path. This ambiguous nature of the Clouds, for whom the play is named, aptly reflects the complex and ambiguous nature of the play as a whole.

Production

Since fifth-century comic poets put on a play for a particular competition and did not envisage future productions, an original script that later circulated as a text for readers contained only the words, with few if any attributions of lines to speaker and no stage directions. These had to be inferred from the words of the text itself, so that all editions and translations, ancient and modern, differ to some extent in reconstructing the theatricality of the text. This means that anyone reading or performing an ancient comedy has a perfect right to bring the text to life in any way that seems appropriate: we have no information external to the text itself about how lines were originally distributed or performed, or about the original action on-stage and in the orchestra. Thus there can be no 'authentic' productions of ancient comedies, only productions that strive, to a greater or lesser degree, to approximate what little we know of performance conditions at the time of their original production. In any case it is pointless to argue about 'authenticity': in the end only satisfied spectators really count.

In this translation I assign speakers who seem to be the likeliest candidates for given lines; the reader is free to differ. I do not, however, supply stage-directions in the text itself: one of the pleasures of reading or performing an ancient comedy is imagining how it might be realized in action. I hesitate to put my own imagination in the way of a reader's, an actor's or a director's. But I do occasionally draw attention, in the notes, to likely action that is not quite obvious from the words of the text.

We do know some facts about fifth-century comic theater, however, and there is no harm in reviewing them for their historical interest.

The actors wore masks, made of cork or papier-mâché, that covered the entire head. These were generic (young man, old woman, etc.) but might occasionally be special, like a portrait-mask of a prominent citizen (Socrates may well have been so caricatured in *Clouds*). Their clothing was contemporary and generically suited to their identities except that, wherever possible, it accommodated the traditional comic features of big stomach and rump and (for men) the phallos, made of leather, either dangling or erect as appropriate, and circumcised in the case of outlandish barbarians. All roles were played by men. The naked women who often appear were men wearing body-stockings to which false breasts and genitalia were attached. The city supplied an equal number of actors to each competing poet, probably three, and these actors played all the speaking roles. In *Birds*, for example, there are 22 speaking roles, but the text's entrances and exits are so arranged that three actors can play them all. Some plays do, however, require a fourth (or even a fifth) actor in small roles. Perhaps in given years the allotment changed, or novices were periodically allowed to take small parts, or the poet or producer could add extra actors at his own expense.

In the orchestra ('dancing space') was a chorus of twenty-four men who sang and danced to the accompaniment of an aulos, a wind instrument that had two recorder-like pipes played simultaneously by a specially costumed player; and there could be other instruments as well. Like actors, members of the chorus wore masks and costumes appropriate to their dramatic identity. There could be dialogue be-

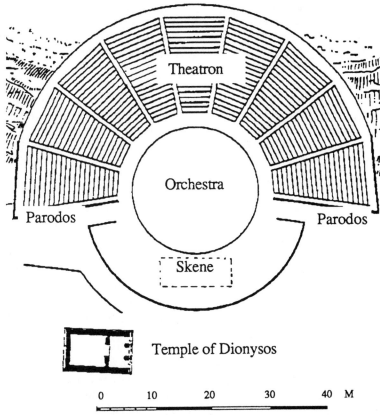

A reconstruction of the theater of Dionysus in Athens during Euripides' career, the second half of the fifth century B.C. (Based on the sketch by J. Travlos, *Pictorial Dictionary of Ancient Athens* [London 1971] 540).

tween the chorus leader and the actors on-stage, but the chorus as a whole only sings and dances. There was no ancient counterpart to the 'choral speaking' often heard in modern performances of Greek drama. The choral songs of comedy were in music and language usually in a popular style, though serious styles were often parodied, and the dancing was expressive, adding a visual dimension to the words and music.

The stage-area was a slightly raised platform behind the large orchestra. Behind it was a wooden two-story building called the *skene* ('tent', from which our word 'scene'). It had two or three doors at stage-level, windows at the second story, and a roof on which actors could appear. On the roof was a crane called the *mechane* ('machine'), on which actors could fly above the stage (as gods, for example, whence the Latin expression *deus ex machina*, 'god from the machine'). Another piece of permanent equipment was a wheeled platform called the *ekkyklema* ('device for rolling out'), on which actors and scenery could be wheeled on-stage from the skene to reveal 'interior' action. A painted or otherwise decorated plywood facade could be attached to the skene if a play (or scene) required it, and movable props and other scenery were used as needed. Since plays were performed in daylight in a large outdoor amphitheater, all entrances and exits of performers and objects took place in full view of the spectators. All in all, more demand was made on the spectators' imagination than in modern illusionistic theater, so that performers must often tell the spectators what they are supposed to see.

A fifth-century comedy was played through without intermission, the performance lasting about two hours. The usual structure of a comedy was a Prologue (actors); the Parodos, or entry, of the chorus into the orchestra (chorus); an Agon, or contest (actors and chorus); the Parabasis, or self-revelation, of the chorus (chorus leader and chorus); and a series of episodes (actors) articulated by choral songs (chorus). In some plays, like *Clouds*, there can be a second parabasis and/or a second agon. In this translation I have supplied appropriate divisions of the action, but performers should, as always, feel free to arrange their own performance as they see fit.

This translation is designed to be perfectly comprehensible to contemporary readers, and the best way to stage it is to make it just as comprehensible to the audience for whom it is to be performed, using whatever human and other resources are available. Balloons, for example, make perfectly good comic phalloi, and music for the songs and moves for the dancers can be as simple or elaborate as one cares to make them. I have translated the songs into standard poetic forms, so that they might be sung to any number of appropriate modern tunes. Adaptations of characters, and insertion of allusions to current events make for liveliness (Aristophanes himself did this). The conflict of generations, the puzzlement of the ordinary person when confronted by arcane knowledge and novel arguments—these seem always relevant and need little adaptation. But if the intended audience has never heard of clasical Athens or of Socrates, a modern producer may insert explanatory material or devise some other topical adaptation without violating any sort of standard of authenticity.

The play is stageworthy; the best guide for performance is the text itself.

Suggestions for Further Reading

Readers interested in the Greek text are referred to the editions with commentary by K.J. Dover (Oxford 1968) and A.H. Sommerstein (Warminster 1982), which has an excellent literal translation.

Readers interested in the philosophical portrayal of Socrates are referred to the works of Plato (especially the *Apology* and the dialogues *Crito, Phaedo, Phaedrus, Republic* and *Symposium*) and Xenophon (especially the *Apology* and the *Memorabilia*).

Ancient information about comedy is collected by A.W. Pickard-Cambridge in *Dithyramb, Tragedy and Comedy*, rev. by T.B.L. Webster (Oxford 1962), and about the theatrical festivals in the same author's *The Dramatic Festivals of Athens*, rev. by J. Gould and D.M. Lewis (Oxford 1968, rev. 1988).

Good general treatments are:

Arnott, P. *Greek Scenic Conventions in the Fifth Century B.C.* (Oxford 1962).
Dover, K.J. *Aristophanic Comedy* (California 1972).
Harriott, R.M. *Aristophanes, Poet and Dramatist* (Baltimore 1986).
Hubbard, T.K. *The Mask of Comedy. Aristophanes and the Intertextual Parabasis* (Ithaca 1991).
McLeish, K. *The Theatre of Aristophanes* (New York 1980).
Moulton, C. *Aristophanic Poetry* (Hypomnemata 68: Göttingen 1981).
Reckford, K.J. *Aristophanes' Old-and-New Poetry* (Chapel Hill 1987).
Sifakis, G. *Parabasis and Animal Choruses* (London 1971).
Stone, L.M. *Costume in Aristophanic Comedy* (New York 1981).
Walcot, P. *Greek Drama in its Theatrical and Social Context* (Cardiff 1976).
Webster, T.B.L. *Greek Theatre Production* (London 1970).
Whitman, C.H. *Aristophanes and the Comic Hero* (Cambridge MA 1964).
Winkler, J.J. and Zeitlin, F.I., edd. *Nothing to Do With Dionysos? Athenian Drama in its Social Context* (Princeton 1990).

Worth reading among the very numerous studies bearing on *Clouds* are:

Adkins, A.H.W. 'Clouds, Mysteries, Socrates and Plato', *Antichthon* 4 (1970) 13-24.
Guthrie, W.K.C. *A History of Greek Philosophy* vol. III (Cambridge 1969) 3-319 (on the sophists).

Havelock, E.A. 'The Socratic Self as it is Parodied in Aristophanes' *Clouds*', *Yale Classical Studies* 22 (1972) 1-18.

Hubbard, T.K. 'Parabatic Self-Criticism and the Two Versions of Aristophanes' *Clouds*', *Classical Antiquity* 5(1986) 182-97.

Kerferd, G.B. *The Sophistic Movement* (Cambridge 1981).

Nussbaum, M. 'Aristophanes and Socrates on Learning Practical Wisdom', *Yale Classical Studies* 26 (1980) 43-97.

Ostwald, M. The Polarizations of the 420s', Ch. 5 in *From Popular Sovereignty to the Sovereignty of Law* (California 1986) 199-290.

Segal, C.P. 'Aristophanes' Cloud-Chorus', *Arethusa* 2 (1969) 143-61.

Silk, M. 'Aristophanes as a Lyric Poet', *Yale Classical Studies* 26 (1980) 99-151.

Strauss, L. *Socrates and Aristophanes* (Chicago 1966).

Vlastos, G. 'Socratic Irony', *Classical Quarterly* 37 (1987) 79-96.

CLOUDS

CHARACTERS

Speaking Characters
Strepsiades, *an old Athenian*
Pheidippides, *Strepsiades' young son*
Slave *of Strepsiades*
Pupils *of Socrates (two)*
Socrates *the philosopher*
Chorus *of Clouds*
The Better Argument
The Worse Argument
First Creditor, *Strepsiades' fellow-villager*
Second Creditor

Mute Characters
Pupils *of Socrates*
Witness *summoned by First Creditor*
Xanthias, *slave of Strepsiades*
Slaves *of Strepsiades*

SCENE I

(Strepsiades, Pheidippides, Slave)

Strepsiades[1]
  Aargh!
  Good God almighty, what a monstrous night!
  It's endless. Will the daylight never come?
  I heard the cock crow quite a while ago,
  but the slaves are snoring. They wouldn't in the old days.   5
  Damn the war, it's messed up lots of things,

---

[1]Though the name Strepsiades is attested of real people, Aristophanes probably chose it because it expresses this character's anxious 'tossing and turning' (*strephei*, 36) over his debts and his subsequent attempts to 'reverse' (*ekstrepson*) his son's life and to 'twist lawsuits' (*strepsodikesai*, 434) to avoid repaying his debts.

when I can't whip my own slaves anymore.[1]
But this fine young man here isn't any better;
he won't get up 'fore daylight, just keeps farting away,
wrapped up in five thick woolly coverlets.   10
Oh, I give up! Let's *all* cover up and snore.
Tarnation! How can I sleep a wink, tormented
by all my bills and stable-fees and debts,
because of my son here, who never gets a haircut,
who's totally into horses and chariot-racing.   15
He even *dreams* about horses! But *I'm* the goner,
always watching the moon phase out the month,
and my credit-rating with it. Boy! Light a lamp,[2]
bring me my ledgers, so I can calculate
how many I owe to, and what the interest is.   20
OK, the bottom line. Twelve grand to Pasias.
Twelve grand to Pasias? Why did I borrow that?
When I bought the horse with the K-brand. What a fool!
I should have had my eye knocked out with a stone.

Pheidippides
Yo Philon! Don't be cheating! Ride in your own lane!   25

Strepsiades
That's it! That's just the kind of crap that's done me in.
He's riding horses even in his sleep!

Pheidippides
How many laps are the war-chariots down to drive?

Strepsiades
It's me, your father, you're driving round the bend!
Well, after Pasias, what's the next IOU?   30
Amynias, three grand for a seat and a set of wheels.

Pheidippides
Groom, roll the horse in the dust, then stable him.

Strepsiades
It's *you*, dear lad, who's been rolling—in *my money*.
And now I've been served papers, and other creditors
are threatening to sue me.

---

[1]During the Peloponnesian war, neighboring Megara and Boeotia were hostile powers and Peloponnesian armies periodically invaded the Attic countryside, so that ill-treated slaves might be tempted to run away from their masters and seek refuge in another land. This would be much harder to do in peacetime, when international agreements discouraged the harboring of runaway slaves.

[2]'Boy' was the conventional way to address a male slave.

Pheidippides

Really, father!   35
Why are you tossing and turning all night long?

Strepsiades
There's a bailiff in the bedclothes biting me.

Pheidippides
What a crazy guy! Please let me catch some sleep.

Strepsiades
Excuse me! Sleep away! But I'm warning you,
one day these debts will all be on *your* back.   40
Gawd.
That matchmaker ought to die a horrible death
for getting me to marry that mother of yours.
I had a mighty good life there, down on the farm,
unwashed, unswept, lying around as I pleased,
brimming with honey-bees, sheep and olive-trees.   45
And then I married the niece of Megacles,[1]
Megacles' son. Farmer weds urbanite,
a snobby, spoiled clothes-horse kind of girl.
When we hitched, I climbed up to the wedding bed
smelling of new wine, figs, fleeces and good produce;   50
while *she* smelled of perfume, saffron, tongue-kisses, expense,
of overeating and Aphrodite's shrines.[2]
I don't say she was lazy; she did her weaving.
I'd show her these pants of mine as evidence
and say, 'Wife, you needn't pack the threads so close.'[3]   55

Slave
The oil in the lamp's run out on us.

Strepsiades
Oh dammit, why'd you light the thirsty lamp?
Come here and take your beating!

Slave
Why *should* I?

---

[1]Although a contemporary Megacles, son of Megacles is known, there is no
apparent reason why we should think particularly of him here; such names
were not uncommon and they connote wealth and aristocratic pedigree.

[2]'Kolias and Genetyllis', divinites associated with Aphrodite, goddess of
sexual enjoyment, and (according to comic poets) a popular gathering-place
for housewives up to no good.

[3]I.e., use so much (expensive) thread in simple mending.

Strepsiades

Because you put in one of the fattest wicks!
And then, when this here boy was born to us,   60
to me and to my high-class wife, that is,
we started yelling at each other about his name.
She wanted a name with *hippus*, meaning *horse*,
Xanthippus or Chaerippus or Callipides,
while I liked Pheidonides, his granddad's name.[1]   65
We compromised and called him Pheidippides.
She used to pick him up and coo at him,
'When you grow up you'll drive a chariot to town,
like Megacles, and wear fine robes'. And I'd say,   70
'No, when you drive the goats home to the barnyard,
like your very own dad, you'll wear a leather jacket'.
But he didn't listen to anything I said,
but gave my wallet a case of the galloping trots.
That's why I've spent the whole night searching for   75
one little path of escape, an excellent miracle-cure.
If I can convince my son, I shall be saved!
But first I've got to get him out of bed.
Now what's the gentlest way for me to wake him?
Pheidippides. Pheidippidoodle.

Pheidippides

What, dad?   80

Strepsiades

Gimme a kiss and show me your right hand.

Pheidippides

OK. What's up?

Strepsiades

So tell me: do you love me?

Pheidippides

By this Poseidon, Lord of Horses, I do.[2]

Strepsiades

Don't give me any of that Poseidon stuff!
That god's the very source of all my troubles!   85
But, if you really love me with all your heart,
please do what I say, my son.

---

[1]'Pheidonides' means 'Thrifty'.
[2]Evidently Pheidippides has a picture or a statue of the horse-god Poseidon
   by his bed.

Pheidippides

          And what is that?

Strepsiades
I'd like you, as soon as possible, to reverse your life,
and go to learn the things I want you to.

Pheidippides
So tell me, what are these 'things'?

Strepsiades

          You'll do it?

Pheidippides

              Sure,   90
by Dionysus, I will.

Strepsiades

          Look over there, then.
You see that little door, that little house?

Pheidippides
I see it. So tell me, dad, just what *is* it?

Strepsiades
That house is a Thinkery for clever souls.
Some gentlemen live there who argue that the sky   95
is a casserole-cover—and make us all believe it—
and that it covers us all, and we're charcoal briquets.[2]
These people train you, if you pay them money,
to win any argument, whether it's right or wrong.

Pheidippides
Who *are* these people?

Strepsiades

          I can't exactly *name* them.   100
Reflective cogitators, upstanding gentlemen.

Pheidippides
Yuk! That scum! I know who you mean. The charlatans,
the pasty-faces, the ones who don't wear shoes,
like that miserable Socrates, and Chaerephon![3]

---

[1]Evidently Pheidippides has a picture or a statue of the horse-god Poseidon
by his bed.

[2]No such theory is attributed to any philosopher outside of comedy; if
anything it is a popular misunderstanding of some cosmogonic theory.

[3]Chaerephon was the long-time friend of Socrates who (according to Plato's
Apology) asked the Delphic oracle if any man was wiser than Socrates. He
was nicknamed 'The Bat' because of his thin, pale countenance, and comic
poets ridiculed him as a thief, an informer and a parasite.

Strepsiades
> Hey now, be quiet! Don't speak childishly.   105
> And have a care about your father's daily bread.
> Lay off the racing and join their company.

Pheidippides
> No way, no, by Dionysus! Not even if you gave me
> those fancy pheasants that Leogoras breeds![1]

Strepsiades
> Come on, I implore you, dearest of all to me,   110
> matriculate.

Pheidippides
>   And what do you want me to study?

Strepsiades
> I'm told they have both kinds of argument:
> the Better, whatever that is, and the Worse.
> And one of these Arguments, the Worse, I'm told,
> can argue even an unjust case and win!   115
> So if you could learn this Worse Argument for *me*,
> then all these debts I owe on your account
> I wouldn't have to pay, not even a penny![2]

Pheidippides
> I just can't. How could I even dare to *look*
> at the Knights with all the tan scraped off my face?   120

Strepsiades
> Then, by Demeter, you've had your last meal here,
> and so's your yoke-horse and your thoroughbred.
> I'm throwing you out of the house, and go to hell!

Pheidippides
> My godlike uncle Megacles won't leave me
> horseless. I'll go to him and pay *you* no mind.[3]   125

---

[1]Leogoras, father of the orator Andocides, was a wealthy aristocrat related to the family of Pericles.

[2]The philosopher Protagoras seems to have been the first to claim that there are always two arguments about any issue and that it is possible for a skilled pleader to make a convincing case for either side, however weak the case may seem to be to the unskilled person. In Plato's *Apology* Socrates complains of his reputation for 'making the worse argument the better' and says that philosophers are always easy targets for such an accusation, just as lawyers are today.

[3]Pheidippides marches off to Megacles' house.

SCENE II

(Strepsiades, Pupil, other Pupils)

Strepsiades
And I won't take this setback lying down.
I'll say a little prayer and go myself
to the Thinkery to get an education.
But how's an old man like me, forgetful and dense,
to learn precise, hair-splitting arguments? 130
I've just *got* to go. What use is procrastination?
Just knock on the door. Hello? Boy! Little boy!

Pupil
Buzz off to blazes! Who's pounding on the door?

Strepsiades
Strepsiades, son of Pheidon, from Cicynna.[1]

Pupil
An ignoramus, I'd say, the way you furiously 135
stomp on the door so inconsiderately,
aborting a cogitation just conceived.[2]

Strepsiades
Forgive me, please, I live way out in the country.
But tell me about the thing that was aborted.

Pupil
It's sacrilege to tell anyone but the pupils. 140

Strepsiades
Go on, don't worry; the man you see before you
has come to the Thinkery to be a pupil too.

Pupil
I'll tell you, then. But these are holy secrets.[3]
This morning Socrates asked Chaerephon
how many of its own feet a flea can jump. 145
A flea had bitten Chaerephon on the eyebrow
and then jumped off and landed on Socrates' head.

---

[1]The full version of an Athenian name; Cicynna was a small, rural and relatively insignificant deme (local community) and was probably chosen by Aristophanes for that reason.
[2]Strepsiades had probably knocked very timidly.
[3]Aristophanes portrays the Thinkery as a kind of mystery-cult, with Socrates as its guru.

Strepsiades
And how did he measure the jump?

Pupil
                              Most cleverly.
He melted wax, then picking up the flea,
he dipped both its little feet into the wax,   150
which, when it cooled, made little Persian slippers.
He took these off and was measuring the distance.

Strepsiades
Good God almighty, what subtlety of mind!

Pupil
That's nothing! Just wait till you hear another idea
of Socrates'. Wanna?

Strepsiades
                              What? Please tell me!   155

Pupil
Our Chaerephon was asking his opinion
on whether gnats produce their humming sound
by blowing through the mouth or through the rump.

Strepsiades
So what did Socrates say about the gnat?

Pupil
He said the gnat has a very narrow gut,   160
and, since the gut's so tiny, the air comes through
quite violently on its way to the little rump;
then, being an orifice attached to a narrow tube,
the asshole makes a blast from the force of the air.[1]

Strepsiades
So a gnat's asshole turns out to be a bugle!   165
Thrice-blesséd man, what enterology!

Pupil
But the other day he lost a great idea
because of a lizard.

Strepsiades
                              Really? Please tell me how.   170

Pupil
He was studying the tracks of the lunar orbit
and its revolutions, and as he skyward gaped,
from the roof in darkness a lizard shat on him.

---

[1]Caricaturing contemporary scientific models that sought to explain the mechanics of hearing.

Strepsiades
Ha ha ha ha. A lizard shitting on Socrates!

Pupil
Then last night we hadn't a thing to eat for dinner.   175

Strepsiades
Aha. So how did he contrive to get your food?

Pupil
Over the table he spread a thin coat of ashes,
and bent a skewer,[1] then picking up a queer
over at the gymnasium, he stole his clothes.

Strepsiades
And why do people still admire Thales?[2]   180
Open up the Thinkery, and make it quick;
I want to see Socrates as soon as possible.
I yearn to learn. Come on now, open up![3]
Good God, what kind of creatures have we here?

Pupil
What's the matter? Do they look strange to you?   185

Strepsiades
They look like prisoners of war, the ones from Sparta.
But why are they peering at the ground like that?

Pupil
Investigating subterranean phenomena.

Strepsiades
                                    I see,
they're after truffles. But you needn't bother with that:
I know where you can find big, tasty ones.   190
But why are these pupils here bent over so?

Pupil
They're scrutinizing the gloomy realms below.

Strepsiades
Then why are their assholes pointing toward the sky?

Pupil
Their assholes are learning astronomy on their own.

[1]As if to perform a scientific or magical procedure.
[2]Thales, the sixth-century founder of Milesian philosophy, had a reputation
for genius and wisdom comparable to Einstein's today.
[3]Stagehands roll out the *ekkyklema*, a wheeled platform kept inside the stagebuilding that was used to reveal what was supposed to be going on inside.
On the *ekkyklema* are a number of pupils and a pegboard on which various
instruments and objects are hung.

But all of you, go in; he mustn't catch you here. 195

Strepsiades
Not yet, not yet! Please let them stay awhile.
I want to tell them a small problem of my own.

Pupil
I'm sorry, they're not allowed to be outside
in the open air for any great length of time.

Strepsiades
Pray tell me what these are, these instruments? 200

Pupil
This here's astronomy.

Strepsiades
                        And what are these?

Pupil
Geometry.

Strepsiades
                        And what's the use of that?

Pupil
For measuring land.

Strepsiades
                        Like land for settlers?

Pupil
All *kinds* of land.

Strepsiades
                        A very urbane device,
both useful and entirely democratic.[1] 205

Pupil
And here we have a map of the whole world. See?
Here's Athens.

Strepsiades
                        What do you mean? I don't believe you.
I don't see any jurors hearing cases.[2]

---

[1]Strepsiades seems to think that geometry is a device for distributing all the
  world's land to Athenians like himself.

[2]The courts, with their large paid juries of ordinary citizens, were Athens'
  principal means of making and enforcing the laws that governed not only
  the Athenians but all members of their empire as well. Because of the
  prominence of the courts in Athenian public life, the Athenians had a
  reputation for being litigious and meddlesome. Aristophanes satirizes
  Athenian juries in his play *Wasps*.

Pupil
Take it from me, this really is Attica.

Strepsiades
Then where's Cicynna and my fellow villagers?   210

Pupil
They're over here. And here, you see, is Euboea,
this area laid out all along the mainland.

Strepsiades
I know: we laid it out ourselves with Pericles.[1]
But where is Sparta?[2]

Pupil
                          Here it is. Over here.

Strepsiades
So close? You'd better think about *that* some more,   215
and move them a whole lot farther away from *us*.

Pupil
Impossible.

Strepsiades
                   Just move it, or, by God, I'll—
Hey, who's that man there hanging in the air?[3]

Pupil
The master.

Strepsiades
                   Master?

Pupil
                          Socrates.

Strepsiades
                          Socrates!
OK you, introduce me, good and loud!   220

Pupil
You call him yourself; I haven't got the time.

---

[1]Twenty-three years earlier Pericles had led an Athenian force to Eubeoa to
  suppress a revolt.
[2]Sparta and her allies were at this time Athens' great enemy in the Peloponnesian War.
[3]Socrates is swung into view on the *mechane* ('machine'), a crane attached to
  the stagebuilding, usually used to bring on heroes or gods (hence the phrase
  deus ex machina). The Socrates of Plato's *Apology* complains of his airborne
  portrayal in our play, saying that people long remembered it and that it
  contributed to his bad reputation as one who despised ordinary people and
  their conventions.

SCENE III

(*Strepsiades, Socrates*)

Strepsiades
Oh Socrates!
Socratikins!

Socrates
Why callest thou, mere mortal?

Strepsiades
First tell me, pray, just what you're doing up there.

Socrates
I tread the air and contemplate the sun.   225

Strepsiades
You're spying on the gods from a wicker basket?
Why can't you do that, if you must, down here?

Socrates
Never
could I make correct celestial discoveries
except by thus suspending my mind, and mixing
my subtle head with the air it's kindred with.   230
If down below I contemplate what's up,
I'd never find aught; for the earth by natural force
draws unto itself the quickening moisture of thought.
The very same process is observable in lettuce.[1]

Strepsiades
How's that?   235
It's thought that draws the moisture into lettuce?
Come down, Socratikins, come down here to me,
so you can teach me what I've come to learn.

Socrates
And what might that be?

Strepsiades
I want to learn oratory.
By debts and interest payments and rapacious creditors   240
I'm assailed and assaulted and stand to lose my property.

---

[1]Caricaturing (and muddling) the ideas of the physicist Diogenes, who studied the role of the wet and the dry in nature. Among Diogenes' theories is one that animals are less intelligent than human beings because the air they breathe, coming from near the ground, is moister and so produces an intellect less 'pure and dry' than ours.

Socrates
So how did you manage to slip into this condition?

Strepsiades
It's an equine ailment that's eating me up alive.
No matter. Teach me one of your Arguments,
the one that pays no debts. Whatever your fee,   245
I'll pay it, I swear by all the gods, in cash.

Socrates
What do you mean, 'the gods'? In the first place, gods
aren't legal tender here.

Strepsiades
              Then how do you swear?
With iron coins, as in Byzantium?

Socrates
You want to know the truth about the gods,   250
what they really are?

Strepsiades
           By God I do, if it's possible.

Socrates
And to enter into communion with the Clouds,
who are our deities?[1]

Strepsiades
           I'd like to very much.

Socrates
Then sit yourself upon the sacred sofa.

Strepsiades
I'm ready.

Socrates
        Very well. Now take hold of this,   255
the wreath.

Strepsiades
        A wreath? Good heavens, Socrates,
you're not going to sacrifice me, like Athamas?[2]

---

[1]No Greek would think of worshipping the clouds; they are 'goddesses' suitable only for the comic Thinkery of Socrates, who teaches men how to obscure reality by making it as changeable and evanescent as the clouds.

[2]Recollecting the scene in Sophocles' play *Athamas* (not extant) in which the hero sits, wreathed, on the altar of Zeus, about to be sacrificed for a wrong he had done to his wife, Nephele (whose name means 'cloud').

Socrates

> Oh no. We perform this ceremony for everyone
> we initiate.

Strepsiades

> But what do *I* get out of it?

Socrates

> You'll be a spieler, a gong, the flower of orators!   260
> Hold still now.[1]

Strepsiades

> Oh my god, I see you weren't joking:
> the way you're dredging me I *will* be flour!

Socrates

> Let the oldster speak with reverence,
>   let him hear our pious prayer.
> Mighty Master, Air unbounded,
>   thou who hold the floating earth;[2]
> Ether bright,[3] and Clouds so awesome,
>   goddesses of thunder loud!   265
> Rise on high, o mistresses,
>   appear to him who thinks on you!

Strepsiades

> Wait until I get my raincoat;
>   I don't want a drenching here!
> What a fool I was to come with
>   nothing, even a simple hat!

Socrates

> Come then, Clouds most glorious, and
>   show yourselves to this man here.
> Whether on the holy snowy
>   peak of Olympus ye now sit,   270
> or nymphs to a holy dance you're calling
>   in father Ocean's garden, or
> whether again in the Nile delta

---

[1]Socrates sprinkles him with flour, like a sacrificial beast.

[2]Ionian philosophers as early as Anaximenes held that the earth was a disc supported by air (one of the four 'elements', along with earth, water and fire); for Aristophanes air (empty and insubstantial) symbolizes the emptiness and insubstantiality of Socratic theories and values.

[3]The 'ether' was thought to lie between the air and the sky; though it was popularly considered to be divine because of its proximity to the gods, the philosophers speculated about its relationship (if any) to the four elements of the biosphere.

you're drawing water in golden bowls,[1]
or hanging out at Lake Maeotis
or up on Mimas' snowy crag:
hearken to my call; accept my
sacrifice;[2] enjoy our rites!

SCENE IV (PARODOS)

(Chorus, Socrates, Strepsiades)

Chorus (I[1])[3]

Clouds everlasting,	275
rise and appear in your radiance dewy,	
rise from your deep-crashing father, the Ocean,	
rise to the towering peaks of the forested mountains!	
Let us look down on the hilltops majestic,	280
down on the holy earth's crops that we rain on,	
rivers resounding in spate divine,	
oceans resounding in thunderous booms!	
Heaven's untiring eye is ablaze	285
with sparkling rays.	
Shake from our deathless shapes the mist of rain;	
look on the earth with telescopic eye!	290

Socrates

Clouds that we revere so greatly,
    show that you have heard my cry!
You: you heard their voice, their thunder,
    bellowing with force divine?

Strepsiades

Honored Clouds, I do revere you;
    let me answer with a fart

---

[1]In Diogenes' theory explaining the Nile's summer flooding, it was the sun (a traditional god) and not the clouds that drew up moisture.

[2]Perhaps Socrates is thinking of Strepsiades as a sort of sacrifice; perhaps he had burned some incense as part of the rigamarole in 260 ff.

[3]The songs and dances performed in the orchestra by a Greek dramatic chorus were normally strophic, i.e. composed in two or more strophes (stanzas) that had the same rhythmical structure. In this translation each chorus is numbered and each strophe comprising a chorus is numbered by superscript; thus the song beginning in line 275 is the first strophe of the first chorus; the second strophe begins in line 299.
The entry song of the chorus (technically called the *parodos*) is unique in Aristophanes in that it is sung offstage: the Clouds do not actually enter the orchestra until 323. This staging is a novel surprise, creates suspense and establishes our feeling for the impermanence, the whimsicality and the untrustworthiness of the Clouds.

all their thunder: that's how scared they've
　　made me, that's how terrified!
Now, if its allowed, or even
　　if it's not, I need to crap!　　　　　　　　　　　　　295

Socrates

Don't be joking, don't behave like
　　one of these comedians!
Reverence, please! A swarm of gods are
　　stirring and prepared to sing.

Chorus (I^2)

Rain-bearing maidens,
come to the glistening land of Athena,　　　　　　　300
Cecrops' soil with its crop of fine he-men;[1]
here is the home of the sanctified rites none may speak of,[2]
the temple in festival open for worship,
gifts for the heavenly gods in abundance,　　　　　305
temples on high, sacred statues and
holy processions and sacrifice,
ubiquitous garlands, festivities here
　　throughout the year.
The onset of spring brings Dionysian joy,　　　　310
maddening dance, the music of the flute.

Strepsiades

Tell me, Socrates, I beg you,
　　who these ladies are that sang
such a reverent song as this? They
　　aren't some kind of heroines?　　　　　　　　315

---

[1]Cecrops was a legendary king of Athens.

[2]The Mysteries of Demeter and Kore, located at Eleusis (about 12 miles from Athens), was an internationally renowned cult that initiated thousands of people annually. The cult's central myth (recounted in the *Homeric Hymn to Demeter*) told of the rape of the daughter (Kore) of Demeter (goddess of crops, especially grain) by Hades (lord of the underworld and brother of Zeus); Demeter's search for Kore, during which no crops were permitted to grow; Demeter's arrival in Attica; the compromise by which Kore is restored to Demeter for part of the year (when crops grow) but spends the remainder (winter) with her husband in the underworld; and the foundation of the Mysteries to commemmorate these events. It was considered sacrilegious (and very bad luck) to defame the Mysteries or to reveal their central acts. The Clouds' emphasis on Athenian reverence for the Mysteries contrasts strikingly with Socrates' contempt for the traditional gods and with his own private 'mysteries', and it prepares us for the revelation in 1452 ff. that the Clouds have come not to support but to punish the impiety of Socrates and the dishonesty of Strepsiades.

Socrates

    Not at all. They're clouds from heaven,
        goddesses for idle men.
    They're the ones who give us judgment,
        dialectic, intelligence,
    fantasy and double-talking,
        eloquence and forceful talk.

Strepsiades

    Just to hear their voices makes my
        very soul take wing and fly,
    makes me long to chop some logic,
        blow some elocutive smoke,   320
    bust big maxims with little maxims,
        counterpoint an argument!
    Time to see the ladies close up;
        I'm ready now, if now's the time!

Socrates

    Look this way, then, toward Mt. Parnes;
        now I see them coming down
    peacefully.

Strepsiades

            Where? Show them to me.

Socrates

    Quite a bunch are coming on
    through the hollow vales and forests,
        to your side.

Strepsiades

            What's going on?   325
    I can't see them.

Socrates

             Look offstage there.

Strepsiades

    Now I think I'm seeing them!

Socrates

    Now you've simply *got* to see them,
        unless you've got pumpkins in your eyes!

Strepsiades

    There they are! O reverend ladies!
        They're settling over everything.

Socrates

    So, you didn't think that they were

goddesses, and disbelieved?

Strepsiades
Right. I thought that they were only
   lots of dew and steam and gas. 330

Socrates
Didn't know that they sustain and
   feed a host of specialists,
sayers of sooth, quack doctors, hairy
   idlers with onyx signet-rings,
writers of chorus-bending screeches,
   phony meteorologists,
doing nothing useful, living
   only to sing about the Clouds?

Strepsiades
That's why they write 'O dire downdraft
   drumming rainclouds radiant',[1] 335
'Locks of hundred-headed Typho',
   'blasting squalls of mighty blow',
'airy scudders crook'd of talon,
   birds breast-stroking up on high',
'rain of waters down from dew-clouds.'
   Then, for poems like that, they get
fine fillets of choicest mullet,
   avian breast of thrush supreme!

Socrates
Thanks to the Clouds; don't they deserve it?

Strepsiades
Tell me, if they're really clouds, 340
what's the reason why they look so
   much like mortal women do?
Sky-clouds don't resemble *these* clouds.

Socrates
What do *they* look like to you?

Strepsiades
Can't exactly say. They *look* like
   balls of wool spread out up there,
not at all like women, no sir;
   these are wearing noses, too.

---

[1]Parodies 'writers of chorus-bending screeches', i.e. the new style of
   dithyramb (a choral song for Dionysus), which explored complex rhythms
   and orchestration and featured colorature singing of florid poetic texts.

Socrates
Answer me a little question.

Strepsiades
Fire away, whatever you like.   345

Socrates
Ever gazed up and seen a cloud that
    looked just like a centaur, or
a wolf, or bull, perhaps a leopard?

Strepsiades
Sure I have; but what's the point?

Socrates
Clouds take any shape they fancy.
    Say they see a shaggy tough,
one of those hairy guys we all know,
    e.g. Xenophantus' son:[1]
they'll make fun of his affectations,
    making centaurs of themselves.   350

Strepsiades
Say they spot a man who steals from
    public funds, as Simon does?

Socrates
They'll expose his character by
    turning into hungry wolves.

Strepsiades
That's why, when yesterday they saw
    Cleonymus who lost his shield,
showing up his cowardice they
    took the shape of running deer![2]

Socrates
Now it's Cleisthenes[3] they've spotted:
    see him? Thus the Clouds are women.   355

---

[1]The tragic and dithyrambic poet, Hieronymous.

[2]Cleonymus was a minor politician often ridiculed in comedy for obesity and gluttony; in *Clouds* and in subsequent comedies he was teased for having thrown away his shield in battle, probably in the Athenian retreat after the battle of Delium in 424.

[3]A man who was beardless, or unable to grow a proper beard, and so was often satirized as effeminate; here the actor playing Socrates points him out in the audience.

Strepsiades

  Hail then, sovereign Ladies! If you've
    ever so favored another man,
  break for me too, Queens almighty,
    a sound that spans the heavens wide!

Chorus Leader

  Greetings, superannuated
    codger, seeking artful words;
  you too, priest of subtlest hogwash,
    tell us what your heart desires.
  You alone we listen to, of
    all the scientists today,   360
  Prodicus[1] excepted, for his
    cleverness and judgment fine.
  You we like because you swagger
    all over town, and roll your eyes,
  barefoot, suffering every kind of
    woe, and proud on our account.

Strepsiades

  Mother Earth, the sound they make! How
    holy, august, wonderful!

Socrates

  These are the only gods, my man; and
    all the rest are fantasies.   365

Strepsiades

  Come now, don't you all consider
    Zeus on high to be a god?[2]

Socrates

  Zeus, you say? Don't kid me! There's no
    Zeus at all.

Strepsiades

                What's that you say?
  Who makes rain, then? That's what I would

---

[1] A Cean philosopher with interests ranging from natural science to semantics and religion.

[2] Zeus, traditionally the king of the Olympian gods, was popularly conceived as the principal weather god: compeller of clouds, maker of rain and storms, and wielder of the thunderbolt, with which he controlled divine enemies and punished human malefactors. Socrates' following explanations of storms, lightning and thunder as natural phenomena connected with the clouds are humorous versions of scientific theories then in circulation, whether or not the historical Socrates involved himself in their study.

like to know right off the bat.

Socrates

Clouds, of course! I'll prove it so by
        arguments irrefutable.
Tell me, have you ever seen it
        raining when there were no clouds?   370
Why can't Zeus produce a rainstorm
        while the clouds are out of town?

Strepsiades

By Apollo, what you say jibes
        well with what you said before.
When it rained I used to think that
        Zeus was pissing through a sieve!
Tell me, though, who makes the thunder:
        that's what makes me shake and quake.

Socrates

Clouds do, when they roll around.

Strepsiades

                                You'll
        stop at nothing! But tell me, how?   375

Socrates

Clouds fill up with lots of water,
        then they're forced to move about,
sagging soddenly with rain, then
        getting heavier perforce,
collide with one another, breaking
        up and making crashing sounds.

Strepsiades

Who is it, though, that starts them moving?
        Isn't that the work of Zeus?

Socrates

Hardly. It's cosmic Vertigo.[1]

Strepsiades

                        What?
Vertigo? I never realized   380
Zeus is gone and in his place this

---

[1]*Dinos*, 'rotation' or 'whirling', was an important feature of Democritus'
atomic theory of the universe; but in everyday usage *dinos* meant a kind of
cup. Possibly (see 1473) such a cup stood outside the Thinkery. Strepsiades
misunderstands Socrates' reference to a cosmic principle and thinks that
the Socratics worship *Dinos* in the way he worships Zeus; the presence of a
dinos (cup) would thus suggest a divine image.

Vertigo's become the king.
Still you've not explained what makes the
    crashing of a thunder-clap.

Socrates

Weren't you listening? I said that when the
    clouds fill up with water, then
collide with one another, they make a
    crash because of their density.

Strepsiades

Who would fall for that? Come on now.

Socrates

I'll use your body to prove my case.   385
Ever gorged yourself with soup at a
    festival, then got a pain
there in your belly, and suddenly it
    starts to make a rumbling noise?

Strepsiades

By Apollo, yes I have! It
    starts to make an awful fuss;
just a bit of soup starts rumbling,
    making awful thunder-sounds,
gently at first—bap bap bap bap—then
    harder—boomba boomba boom—   390
then I shit and really thunder—
    whamba wham—just like the clouds!

Socrates

Just consider what a fart your
    little belly can produce;
don't you think the boundless air
    produces mighty thunder-claps?
That's in fact the reason why we
    say a fart is breaking wind.

Strepsiades

Tell me this, though: where does lightning
    come from, with its blaze of fire,   395
making us a heap of ash, or
    sometimes merely singeing us?
Plainly that's the weapon used by
    Zeus to punish perjurers.

Socrates

What a moron! You're a throwback,
    truly a neanderthal.

Punish perjurers? Then how come
    Simon isn't lightning-struck?
Or Cleonymus, or Theorus?
    They're as perjured as can be!   400
No, instead he usually zaps his
    very own temple at Sunion,
his own great oak-trees too. What for? The
    oak-trees can't be perjurers!1

Strepsiades
I can't say. You've got a point, though.
    So, what *is* a thunderbolt?

Socrates
When a dry wind lifts aloft and
    gets locked up inside these clouds,
inflating them like big balloons, it
    causes them by natural force   405
to burst; the wind's borne out in a whoosh by
    dint of compressive density,
burning itself entirely up by
    friction and velocity.

Strepsiades
I had the same experience
    myself at Zeus' festival,
roasting a sausage for my kinsmen:
    I forgot to make a slit;
suddenly it bloated up and
    bam! went off just like a bomb,   410
singeing both my eyebrows off and
    covering my face with guts!

Chorus Leader
Creature who desires from us
    magnitudes of cleverness,
blesséd shall you be in Athens,
    blesséd too in all of Greece:
if you have a memory, *if* you
    like to think, and have a hardy
soul, and don't get tired standing
    still or when you walk about,   415
don't mind freezing cold too much, or
    doing without between-meal snacks,
or staying away from wine and stupid

1Oak trees were considered sacred to Zeus.

> things like manly exercise,
> thinking that it's best to have what's
>   fitting for a clever man:
> success as a doer and a counselor
>   and a warrior of the tongue![1]

Strepsiades

> Never fear: my soul is hard, I'm
>   used to brooding through sleepless nights,   420
> my belly's thrifty and lined with iron,
>   used to eating terrible grub.
> These are my credentials, and I'm
>   ready for hammering into shape.

Socrates

> Promise that you'll recognize no
>   god but those *we* recognize,
> Emptiness and Clouds and Tongue, the
>   one and only Trinity?

Strepsiades

> Even if I met the other
>   gods I wouldn't speak to them,   425
> or sacrifice or pour libations
>   or burn the incense on their altars.

Chorus Leader

> Tell us what you'd have us do, then.
>   Speak up, you'll be quite alright,
> if you honor and revere us,
>   if it's cleverness you seek.

Strepsiades

> Sovereign Ladies, all I want from
>   you is something very small:
> to beat the greatest orator in
>   Greece by at least a hundred miles.   430

Chorus Leader

> That we'll give you: in the future
>   none will carry more motions than you.

Strepsiades

> Not for me, no motions, please! I
>   don't desire political clout,

---

[1]These qualities are all attested for the historical Socrates except for abstinence from wine (characteristic of orators in training for a speech) and avoidance of manly exercise (Socrates was an avid wrestler).

just the power of twisting lawsuits,
 and giving my creditors the slip.

Chorus Leader
 That you'll have if that's your pleasure;
  what you want is no big deal.   435
 Now come forth and with confidence
  commit yourself to our agents here.

Strepsiades
 Here I go, with faith in you. And
  anyway I've got no choice:
 those thoroughbred horses and spendthrift wife
  have put me on the brink of ruin.

 Now I'm totally in *their* hands;
 I'll do whatever they might command,   440
 suffer beatings, hunger, thirst,
 flagellation, freezing, dearth.
 Only let me shirk my debts
 and gain renown as the very best
 pusher, spieler, bastard, wheel,   445
 artful liar, total heel,
 shyster, con-man, fount of words,
 loophole, fox, plea-copper, turd,
 slippery liar, shifty skunk,
 loathsome villain, pesty punk,   450
 master-chef of total bunk.

 If people think me all of these,
 let the Thinkers do as they please;
 let them grind me for baloney
 to put on the students' macaroni.   455

Chorus (2)
 He's got intestinal fortitude,
 a bold, ambitious attitude.
 Study hard and play our game,
 and you shall win immortal fame.   460

Strepsiades
 Tell me what's in store for me.

Chorus
 You'll live with us for eternity,
 a paradigm of prosperity.   465

Strepsiades
 Is that what I will really be?

Chorus
>Imagine throngs of clients at your door,
>imploring your advice and consultation   470
>on cases worth a million bucks or more,
>a worthy outlet for your cogitation.   475

Chorus Leader
>Now it's time to test the old man's
>   elementary aptitude;
>diagnose his mental fitness,
>   try his base intelligence.

Socrates
>Now, tell me what your disposition is:
>I need to know so I can bring to bear
>the latest pedagogical artillery.   480

Strepsiades
>How's that? You wanna make war on me? My god!

Socrates
>No, no. I only want some basic info,
>like, how's your memory?

Strepsiades
>   Well, I've got two kinds:
>if someone owes me money, it's very good;
>but if it's me that owes, it's awful bad.   485

Socrates
>Well, are you naturally gifted as a talker?

Strepsiades
>A gifted speaker? No. A deadbeat? Yes.

Socrates
>Then how do you expect to learn?

Strepsiades
>   Just fine.

Socrates
>Alright. I'm going to throw you clever bits
>of cosmological lore; you snap them up.   490

Strepsiades
>I have to eat my lessons like a dog, eh?

Socrates
>The man's an ignoramus, a barbarian!
>Old man, I fear you're going to need a whipping.
>Let's see now: someone hits you, what then?

Strepsiades

Hits me?   495

I play dead, then I summon witnesses,
and after a little while I go to court.

Socrates

OK, remove your shirt.

Strepsiades

Have I been bad?

Socrates

No, candidates must disrobe before they enter.

Strepsiades

But I'm not after stolen goods in there![1]

Socrates

Take it off, stop horsing around.

Strepsiades

So tell me,   500

if I study hard and pay real close attention,
which of your disciples will I be like?

Socrates

You'll be the spitting image of Chaerephon.[2]

Strepsiades

Good heavens no! I'll look just like a zombie!

Socrates

Stop chattering now, and follow me inside.   505
And make it snappy!

Strepsiades

Put pennies on my eyes
before I enter: I'm absolutely terrified
of this descent into the underworld![3]

Socrates

Get going! Stop this skulking on the threshold!

---

[1]Citizens who claimed that their belongings had been stolen could search the
suspect's house, but only if they removed any clothing that might enable
them to bring in something to plant. Strepsiades' protestation would be
insulting to any honest citizen.

[2]See line 104.

[3]In the Greek, 'put a honey cake into my hands...into the cave of Trophonius.'
The hero Trophonius had a subterranean oracular shrine at Lebadeia (in
Boeotia) in which there were sacred snakes; those who entered the cave to
experience prophetic visions took along a honey cake to placate the snakes.

PARABASIS[1]

(Chorus)

Chorus

 All the best of luck to you: 510
 you've shown us lots of derring-do!
 I wish that man felicity,
 for, though far gone in senility,   515
 he's taken the plunge into novelty
 and set his course for sophistry!

Chorus Leader

 You spectators, I will openly speak my mind and tell you
 the truth, I swear by Dionysus who nurtured me.[2]
 As I hope to win the prize and be deemed a skillful poet, 520
 I took you for an audience of great intelligence
 and took this play to be my most sophisticated,
 considering you most worthy to taste it first,[3] a play
 I worked on extra hard. And then I lost the contest,
 defeated undeservedly by vulgar men.[4] Your fault,   525
 you clever ones, whom I took the extra trouble to please!

---

[1]The *parabasis* (self-revelation) of the chorus is a standard feature of Old Comedy that allowed the poet, through speeches by the chorus leader, to address, and also to admonish, the spectators about any issues he cared to raise, whether or not they were directly relevant to the issues raised in the rest of the play. Our parabasis was written for a new version of the play some five years after its first performance (see Introduction); what had been in the parabasis-speech of the original version we do not know. There is a second, more rudimentary, parabasis later in the play (1115 ff).

 The chorus leader (speaking for Aristophanes) first defends the virtues of the original play and blames its failure on the spectators' lack of artistic refinement and on their preference for the less sophisticated work of his rivals. Then, resuming his identity as the Leader of the Cloud chorus, he delivers two *epirrhemes* (responding speeches of 20 lines each) introduced by two responding songs by the Chorus, in which he upbraids the spectators as the Clouds or the Moon might do if they could express political grievances. This structure—*ode, epirrheme* followed by their responsional *antode* and *antepirrheme*—is technically known as an epirrhematic syzygy (*epirrhemes* 'yoked together' by songs).

[2]Dionysus was the patron-god of the theater and therefore of dramatic poets.

[3]He might have produced it at another Athenian festival, or even abroad (though there is no hard evidence that comedies in this period were produced outside Athens, as tragedies could be).

[4]In the contest of 423, *Clouds* came in third (and last) behind Cratinus' *Wine-Flask* and Ameipsias' *Konnos*.

But even so I'll never willingly desert you.
Because here my Good Boy and my Punk[1] were recommended
by certain gentlemen whom it's an honor even to speak of.[2]
I was still a maiden, not yet allowed to have a child,   530
so I exposed my child, and another girl picked it up for me,
and you made sure that it was reared and educated generously.[3]
Since then I've been able to count on your favorable verdict.[4]
So now, like the famous Electra of old, this new comedy
has come in quest of some similarly intelligent spectators: 535
she'll recognize, if she sees it, the lock of her brother's hair.[5]
Just see how modest is her nature! First of all,
she hasn't come all fitted out with a dangling phallus,
red at the end and thick, a joke for little boys;[6]
she doesn't ridicule bald men, or dance lewd dances,   540
or feature an aged protagonist with a walking-stick
that he bashes on whomever's around, thus hiding his terrible
    jokes;
she doesn't run on with torches, or yell 'ow ow ow ow'.
Not she! This comedy trusts in herself and in her script.
And I'm the same kind of poet myself: don't act like a
    bigwig,[7]   545

---

[1]The main characters in Aristophanes's first play, *Banqueters*, which was
produced in 427 and won the second prize. In that play, a traditionally-
minded landowner has two sons, the Good Boy (who has had a traditional
athletic-musical education) and the Punk (who has dropped out of school
to learn the new sophistic methods); their contrasting styles of life provided
an opportunity, as in *Clouds*, to criticize the 'new education'.

[2]I.e. influential patrons had helped the neophyte poet win a place in the comic
contest.

[3]I.e. Aristophanes was then too young to be entrusted with a comic production on his own; an experienced producer (Callistratus or possibly Philo-
nides, both of whom were later to produce other plays by Aristophanes)
took on the job; and the people of Athens sponsored the training of the play's
performers.

[4]*Clouds* was Aristophanes's first failure to win either the first or the second
prize.

[5]Alluding to the recognition-scene in Aeschylus' *Libation-Bearers*, where Electra comes to the tomb of her father Agamemnon and recognizes there a lock
of her long-lost brother's hair.

[6]Aristophanes does is not denying that the male characters in *Clouds* wore the
phallus (a standard accoutrement in comedy), only that none wore the
grotesquely large, circumcised phallus characteristic of barbarians. Young
boys were a prominent element of the theater audience.

[7]The Greek *komo* means both 'wear my hair long' and 'be stuck up'; Aristophanes was prematurely bald.

don't try to fool you by using the same jokes two or three times.
I'm skilled at introducing new ideas every time out,
each one different from the other and all of them good.
I'm the one who hit almighty Cleon with an uppercut,
but I wasn't so brazen as to hit him again when he was
    down.[1]   550
Not so my rivals: once they got a hold of Hyperbolus,
they've never stopped stomping the poor man, and his mother
    too.[2]
First there was Eupolis, dragging his *Maricas* onto the stage,
a cheap and incompetent rehash of my own play, *Knights*,[3]
adding to it only the drunken crone dancing lewdly,   555
Phrynichus' old joke, when the sea-monster tried to eat her.[4]
Then Hermippus entered the parade against Hyperbolus,[5]
and now all the others are launching into Hyperbolus too,[6]

---

[1]Cleon was the most influential politician in Athens after the death of Pericles in 429. In 426 Aristophanes had attacked him in his play, *Babylonians*, and again in 424 in his play, *Knights*; both times Cleon had subsequently tried to prosecute him. It is not true that Aristophanes spared Cleon after his death in 422: he attacked him in *Peace* (produced in 421) and attacks him again later in this very *parabasis* (a holdover from the first version of the play).

[2]The popular politician Hyperbolus, said to have made his fortune in the lamp-making business, assumed Cleon's political position after Cleon's death. In Athenian politics, attacks on an opponent's wife or mother were an accepted competitive technique. Aristophanes himself would later insult Hyperbolus' mother, in *Women at the Thesmophoria* (produced in 411).

[3]Eupolis and Aristophanes were contemporaries and the leading comic poets of their generation. In Eupolis' play (produced in 421) the title character, Maricas, was a barbarian slave representing Hyperbolus, just as the barbarian slave, Paphlagon, had represented Cleon in Aristophanes's *Knights*. No evidence contradicts Aristophanes's frequent claim to have invented this type of 'demagogue-comedy', and Eupolis could counter it only by claiming to have contributed ideas to *Knights*.

[4]In *Maricas* the old crone represented Hyperbolus' mother. Phrynichus the comic poet was a contemporary of Aristophanes and Eupolis. He had apparently used the crone in a parody of the myth of Andromeda, the beautiful princess whom Perseus rescued from a sea-monster. Later, in *Women at the Thesmophoria* (produced in 411), Aristophanes would parody the same myth, but he substituted an old man for Andromeda.

[5]An older contemporary of Aristophanes who attacked Hyperbolus and his mother in the play, *Breadsellers*, produced in 420 or 419.

[6]The comic dramatist Plato wrote a play entitled *Hyperbolus*, and probably there were (as Aristophanes claims) others as well, though we have no record of them.

all of them copying my own similes about the eels.[1]
Think *they're* funny? You better not enjoy *my* plays then!   560
But if you like me and the material I think up,
posterity will consider you to have had good taste!

Chorus (3[1])

Zeus, who rule the gods on high,
you're the first celebrity
invited to our dance.   565

Next Poseidon, mighty keeper
of the trident, savage shaker
of the earth and the briny sea.

Then our famous father, Sky,
nourisher of every life;   570
then our charioteer, the Sun,
illuminating everyone,

for the gods above a mighty force,
for mortals, too, upon the earth.

Chorus Leader

Spectators and critics, give an ear to what I say.   575
We've a gripe against you, and we'll lodge it openly.
Of all the gods we do the most good for this city,
but we're the only gods that get no sacrifices,
no libations, though we look out for you. Whenever
you marshal a stupid expedition, we rain and thunder.[2]   580
When you went to vote for the god-hated tanner Paphlagon,[3]
in the election for generals, we knitted our brows together
and made a lot of noise with lightning and thunderbolts,
and the Moon eclipsed herself from orbit,[4] and the Sun
pulled his blazing wick right back into his lamp   585

---

[1]Referring to *Knights* 864-67, where Paphlagon (Cleon) is compared to a sniggler who likes to fish in troubled waters (i.e. as dishonest politicians flourish in a climate of war and political instability).

[2]I.e. as a bad omen; rain and thunder were in fact reasons to suspend deliberations in the popular Assembly and could sometimes be taken into account when deciding military actions.

[3]I.e. Cleon, whom Aristophanes had portrayed in *Knights* as a Paphlagonian slave and whose wealth at least in part derived from a leather-works. A few weeks after the performance of *Knights* (in February 424) the Athenians elected Cleon as one of the ten generals to hold office the following year.

[4]On 9 October 425, about four months before the election.

and refused to shine on you if you elected Cleon.[1]
But you went ahead and elected him. They say your city
is always making bad decisions, but the gods will always
see that all is well, whatever mistakes you make.
We'll easily show you how to fix this blunder too: 590
convict that vulture Cleon for theft and bribery,
then grab his neck and lock it in the wooden stocks.
Then everything will be as it was before you made
your error, and the city will be on course again.[2]

Chorus (3^2)

Lord of Delos, also join us,   595
Phoebus Apollo, high on Cynthus'
escarpment of sheer rock.

Blesséd Artemis too, who holds in
Ephesus a house all golden,
whom the Lydian girls revere.   600

Goddess of our native land,
Athena, city-guardian,
aegis-wielder, please draw nigh,
and you who haunt Parnassus high,

where torches blaze and maenads stir,   605
Lord Dionysus, reveller!

Chorus Leader

As we prepared to set off on our journey here,
the Moon by chance ran into us and said she wanted
to say hello to all the Athenians and their allies,
but she's most annoyed at your treating her so shamefully   610
despite her many evident and actual benefactions.
First off, she saves you at least ten bucks a month in torches:
that's why you all can say, when you go out in the evening,
No need to buy a torch, my boy, the moonlight's fine!
She says she helps in other ways too. But you don't keep   615
your calendar correct; it's totally out of sync.
As a result, the gods are always getting mad at her,

---

[1]Referring to the solar eclipse of 21 March 424, a few weeks after the election.
Aristophanes might have added that there was an earthquake a few days
after the eclipse, but earthquakes (associated with the sea and earth god
Poseidon) were not in the Clouds' power to initiate.

[2]Since Cleon died in 422, before Aristophanes revised *Clouds*, this *epirrheme*,
which speaks of him as still holding office, must be a relic of the original
version of 423.

whenever they miss a dinner and hungrily go home
because you're celebrating their festival on the wrong day,
or hearing cases or torturing slaves instead of sacrificing.[1]   620
And often, when we gods are mourning Memnon or Sarpedon,[2]
you're pouring wine and laughing. That's why Hyperbolus,
this year's sacred ambassador, had his wreath of office
blown off his head by us gods, so that he'll remember well   625
that the days of your lives should be reckoned by the Moon.[3]

SCENE V

(Socrates, Strepsiades)

Socrates

By Respiration, by Emptiness, by Air,
I've never seen a man so rustic anywhere,
such a clueless, brain-dead case of Alzheimer's!
I give him a teeny table-scrap of knowledge,   630
but he can't remember it long enough to learn it!
I'll call him out of doors here, into the light.
Where are you, Strepsiades? Come out here. Bring your bed.

Strepsiades

I can't; the bugs refuse to let me move it.

Socrates

Right now! And pay attention.

Strepsiades

                      There you are.   635

Socrates

Alright then, what's the first thing you would learn,
of all the things you never learned? Come now,
will it be measures, or diction, or rhythms perhaps?

---

[1]The archon, a public magistrate, was in charge of the official calendar, whose months were often out of strict synchronization with the moon. Sometimes the archon inserted intercalary days into a given month to achieve synchronization or to postpone such events as a periodic festival in honor of a god or gods. In our passage, the gods plan their calendar by the Moon and so blame her when an expected festival (and sacrifice) is not held on the appointed day; but, as the Moon maintains, that is rather the fault of the Athenians' manipulation of the calendar.

[2]Two sons of Zeus (by mortal women) who were killed in the Trojan War.

[3]Hyperbolus had probably called for a vote authorizing an intercalation resulting in the postponement of a regularly scheduled sacrifice; apparently his official wreath of office (as sacred emissary to the Amphictyonic Council, a panhellenic religious body that controlled temples at Thermopylae and Delphi) was blown off by the wind on some public occasion.

Strepsiades
　　Oh, measures for me, 'cause just the other day
　　a grocer shortchanged me two whole liters of flour.　　　640

Socrates
　　Not *that* sort of measure! But what *poetic* measure
　　do you favor, the three-measure or the four-measure lines?

Strepsiades
　　For me, the gallon measure can't be beat.

Socrates
　　You're talking rubbish!

Strepsiades
　　　　　　　　　　　　You wanna bet
　　the gallon isn't made of four quart-measures?　　　645

Socrates
　　To hell with you, you cloddish ignoramus!
　　Perhaps you have an aptitude for rhythms.

Strepsiades
　　But how will rhythms help me make a living?

Socrates
　　First of all, it's socially sophisticated
　　to be able to discriminate between　　　650
　　parade-ground rhythms, say, or the fingered kind.

Strepsiades
　　The fingered kind? That one I know.

Socrates
　　　　　　　　　　　　　　So show me.

Strepsiades
　　Let's see, it's got to be this finger. Yes,
　　when I was a little boy it went like this.[1]

Socrates
　　You stupid lout!

Strepsiades
　　　　　　　　　Look here, you silly goose,　　　655
　　I don't want to learn that stuff.

Socrates
　　　　　　　　　　What *would* you learn?

Strepsiades
　　That thing you teach, you know, that Worsest Argument.

---

[1]Strepsiades gives Socrates the finger.

Socrates
But first you need preliminary studies,
like which quadrupeds are in the masculine gender.

Strepsiades
I know which ones are masculine, all right: 660
the ram, the billygoat, the bull, the dog, the duck.

[Socrates
And the feminine?

Strepsiades
                                        Ewe, she-goat, cow, bitch, and duck.]¹

Socrates
You see what you've done? You call the female duck
a 'duck', and you call the male duck 'duck' as well.

Strepsiades
So what?

Socrates
                        I mean, you call them both a duck.

Strepsiades
I do, by god. And what should I say instead?   665

Socrates
The male's a 'duck', while the female is a 'duchess'.

Strepsiades
A duchess! That's a good one, by the Air!
For that one little lesson alone I swear
I'll fill your thermos up with duchess soup!

Socrates
But there you go again. You give the thermos   670
the masculine gender; it's feminine.

Strepsiades
                                        How do you mean,
I call a thermos masculine?

Socrates
                        Just the way
you say Cleonymus.²

---

¹After line 661 a line has been lost which, as Socrates' response in 662-63
shows, must have contained what the supplement (in brackets) supplies.
²For Cleonymus see 353 n. For the Greeks, cowardice in battle suggested
effeminacy or slavishness, the basis for the following jokes about Cleonymus' 'gender'.

Strepsiades

And how is that?

Socrates

You confuse the endings of thermos and Cleonymus.[1]

Strepsiades

Dear fellow, Cleonymus doesn't have a thermos;   675
to fill him up you simply use his can!
But how should I say thermos properly?

Socrates

How?

You say 'thermé', like the woman's name 'Sostratè'.

Strepsiades

So, thermé feminine?

Socrates

That is quite correct.

Strepsiades

And I should say 'Cleonymè has no thermè'?   680

Socrates

Now let's go on to the following lesson: names,
which ones are masculine, which are feminine.

Strepsiades

I know which ones are feminine.

Socrates

Tell me then.

Strepsiades

Lysilla, Philinna, Clitagora, Demetria.

Socrates

And which are masculine?

Strepsiades

Millions of them are: 685
Philoxenus, Melesias, Amynias.

Socrates

You rascal, those aren't masculine names at all!

Strepsiades

You say they're not?

Socrates

Not masculine at all.

---

[1]In Greek most nouns ending in *-os* are masculine in gender, but a few (like *kardopos*, 'kneading-trough', translated here by 'thermos') are feminine.

Look, how would you greet Amynias if you saw him?

Strepsiades
I'd use the vocative, 'Hi there, Amynia'. 690

Socrates
You see? You used the feminine ending there.

Strepsiades
But isn't that appropriate for a draft dodger?
But why learn things that everybody knows?

Socrates
Oh, never mind. Get into bed.

Strepsiades
                    Why bed?

Socrates
To contemplate a problem of your own. 695

Strepsiades
Oh please, I beg you, not in that bed! I'd rather
lie on the ground to think, if that's OK.

Socrates
There's no alternative.

Strepsiades
                    Now I'm really done for!
The bugs are gonna take it out on my hide today!

SCENE VI

(Duet: Strepsiades and Chorus)

Chorus (4[1])
Cerebrate and contemplate, 700
oscillate and agitate,
in hyperkinetic ratiocination!

No mental snag
should be a drag;
you simply move
to another groove.

Sleep is good for relaxation,
but terrible for speculation! 705

Strepsiades
Ow! Ouch!

Chorus
How dost thou suffer? Wherefore this yelling?

Strepsiades
I'm perishing wretchedly! In this little bed
some Brobdingnagian bugs are biting me,   710
chomping my flank,
draining my gut,
pulling my crank,
poking my butt,
and altogether killing me!   715

Chorus
Yet be thou in thy grief not overzealous

Strepsiades
Easy for you to say, when I'm the one
who's lost his dough,
his suntan too,
who's lost his soul,
can't find his shoes!

Thus suffering   720
in a darkened room,
I lie and sing,
but pretty soon
I fear I'll lose *myself*!

SCENE VII

(Socrates, Strepsiades, Chorus Leader, Chorus)

Socrates
Hey, what are you doing? Aren't you thinking?

Strepsiades
                                          Me?

I am, by god.

Socrates
                    And what have you come up with?

Strepsiades
Wondering how much of me these bugs will eat.   725

Socrates
Oh, go to hell!

Strepsiades
                    I'm already there, dear sir!

Chorus Leader
Don't soften on us! Cover up your head
and think of something thoroughly fraudulent
and scammish.

Strepsiades
>   Damn, I wish someone would give me
> a crooked idea instead of this coverlet!   730

Socrates
> All right, let's see what the fellow's doing now.
> Hey you! Are you asleep?

Strepsiades
>   Good heavens no!

Socrates
> Got hold of something?

Strepsiades
>   Nothing.

Socrates
>   Nothing at all?

Strepsiades
> Nope. All I've got ahold of is my dick.

Socrates
> Then cover your head and think of something quick!   735

Strepsiades
> But what? You tell me something, Socrates.

Socrates
> Tell me what you'd most like to discover.

Strepsiades
> You've heard what I want at least a thousand times!
> My debts! I want to get out of paying them!

Socrates
> All right then, cover up, and slice your mind   740
> into slivers; examine the problem piece by piece,
> sorting it systematically.

Strepsiades
>   Ow! Ouch!

Socrates
> Be quiet! If one idea doesn't work,
> then toss it aside and move along, then later
> try putting that idea in play again.   745

Strepsiades
> Socratikins, my darling!

Socrates
>   What, old man?

Strepsiades
I've found a crooked scheme for evading debts!

Socrates
I'm all ears.

Strepsiades
       Here we go.

Socrates
             Let's hear it then!

Strepsiades
I buy a voodoo woman from Thessaly,
and get her to pull the moon down from the sky,   750
and hide it in a hatbox, like a mirror,
and then make sure that nobody can find it—

Socrates
And how would that be any use?

Strepsiades
            It's easy!
The moon doesn't rise, the month would never end,
and bills would never come due!

Socrates
           Why wouldn't they?   755

Strepsiades
Because you pay your bills on the first of the month!

Socrates
Not bad! But here's another problem for you.
Let's say somebody sues you for a million:
how do you make that lawsuit go away?

Strepsiades
Hmm. Hmm. You've got me there. I need some time.   760

Socrates
Don't wind your thoughts up like a ball of string,
but reel them out a little at a time,
as if you had a cockroach on a leash.

Strepsiades
I've found a brilliant way to bury that lawsuit!
Even you will have to admit it!

Socrates
            Well?   765

Strepsiades
Have you ever seen that stone at the sorcerer's shop,

the beautiful stone that you can see right through,
the one that starts a fire?

Socrates
You must mean glass.

Strepsiades
That's it! So look: if I got some of that stuff,
and watched for the clerk to file my case at court,   770
just standing around, like this, with my back to the sun,
I could zap my case clean off the record books!

Socrates
Very good, by the Graces!

Strepsiades
Gosh, I'm feeling good!
I've erased a lawsuit for a million bucks!

Socrates
All right then, snap up this one.

Strepsiades
Fire away!   775

Socrates
Now: tell how you'd defend yourself against
a case you were losing for lack of witnesses.

Strepsiades
That's nothing; very simple.

Socrates
Yes?

Strepsiades
I'll tell you:
when just one case was pending ahead of mine,
before they called me I'd run off and hang myself.   780

Socrates
What rubbish!

Strepsiades
On the contrary, by god:
no one would take me to court if I were dead!

Socrates
Absurd. Get out! I'm resigning as your teacher.

Strepsiades
But why? By all the gods, dear Socrates!

Socrates
But everything you learn you quite forget.   785

Like, what was your first lesson? Can you tell me?

Strepsiades

All right then, lesson one. What was it now?
The feminine thing we use to carry soup?
Oh damn, what was it?

Socrates

           Go to blazes, you,
you sieve-brained idiotic little old man!   790

Strepsiades

Oh dear! *Now* what will happen to poor old me?
If I can't learn tongue-twisting I'm a goner.
You Clouds, please help me with some good advice.

Chorus Leader

Old man, we're ready to give you some advice.
If you've got a son who's fully raised and grown,   795
send *him* to school to learn instead of you.

Strepsiades

I have a son, a fine young gentleman, too,
but he refuses to learn, so what am I to do?

Chorus Leader

And you give in?

Strepsiades

           He's healthy and well-built,
the scion of high-flown women, Coesyra's clan.[1]   800
But I'll go fetch him, and if he still says no,
I'll absolutely throw him out of the house.
So wait for me here a little while, please.[2]

Chorus (4^2)

Great rewards are on their way
from us to you this very day,   805
for Socrates wants to do whatever you ask him.

Ho, Socrates:
he's on his knees;
you can hear him cluck
like a sitting duck.   810

Better pluck him while you're able:
schemes like yours are quite unstable.

---

[1]Coesyra of Eretria (who claimed descent from Zeus) was the wealthy grand-
mother of Strepsiades' wife (see line 46).
[2]Probably addressed to Socrates.

SCENE VIII

(*Strepsiades, Pheidippides, Socrates*)

Strepsiades
Get out! By Fog, you're welcome here no more!
Go eat the columns of Megacles' mansion!   815

Pheidippides
Good heavens, father, what's the matter with you?
By Zeus on Olympus, your mind has come unhinged.

Strepsiades
Just listen to him! Zeus on Olympus! Stupid!
Believing in Zeus, a boy as old as you!

Pheidippides
And what's so funny about that?

Strepsiades
                                I'm only thinking   820
how babyish you are and how old-fashioned.
But anyway, come here, if you're interested:
I'll tell you a secret that'll make a man of you.
But promise not to share it with anyone.

Pheidippides
All right. What secret?

Strepsiades
                                You just swore by Zeus?   825

Pheidippides
I did.

Strepsiades
        Now look what education does:
there is, Pheidippides, no Zeus.

Pheidippides
                                No Zeus?

Strepsiades
No! Zeus has been dethroned by Vertigo.

Pheidippides
Psh! Now you're raving.

Strepsiades
                                That's the way it is.

Pheidippides
Who told you that?

Strepsiades
> The Melian, Socrates,1   830
and Chaerephon, the flea-footologist.

Pheidippides
You've gone so absolutely bonkers that
you trust those bilious quacks?

Strepsiades
> You watch your mouth!
And don't make light of gentlemen so ingenious
and sensible, so frugal that not one   835
of them has ever had a haircut, ever oiled
himself, or even had a bath. While *you've*
been taking me to the cleaners like a wastrel.
So get a move on and take my place at school!

Pheidippides
But what could I learn from them that's any use?   840

Strepsiades
Oh really? The sum and total of human wisdom!
Find out how thick and ignorant you really are!
Just wait right here a minute; don't go away.

Pheidippides
Good lord, what now? My father's off his rocker.
I could take him to court and have him judged insane,   845
or report his madness to the coffin-makers.

Strepsiades
OK now: tell me, what's the word for this?

Pheidippides
A duck.

Strepsiades
> All right. And what's the word for this?

Pheidippides
A duck.

Strepsiades
> The same for both? You *are* a joke!

1Socrates was a native Athenian; by having Strepsiades refer to him as 'the Melian' Aristophanes alludes to Diagoras of Melos, author of a sophistic proof of the nonexistence of the gods. Around the time Aristophanes was revising *Clouds* Diagoras was accused in the Athenian Assembly of having defamed the Eleusinian Mysteries and was declared an outlaw, with a large bounty being put on his head.

You better stop doing that! This one here is called 850
a duck, while this one here is called a duchess!

Pheidippides

A duchess? Is that the cleverness you learned
in your recent sojourn with those scums of the earth?

Strepsiades

All that and more! But every lesson I learned
I right away forgot. I'm just too old. 855

Pheidippides

I guess that's also how you lost your shirt.

Strepsiades

I didn't lose it, I invested it in knowledge.

Pheidippides

And what about your shoes, you simpleton?

Strepsiades

As Pericles said, you spend what you have to spend[1]
Come on, let's go. Get moving. Humor your father, 860
even if it's wrong. I've done the same for you—
remember?—you were a whining six-year-old,
and the very first buck I made for jury-service
you made me spend on a toy car at the festival.

Pheidippides

You'll live to regret this, dad, just mark my words! 865

Strepsiades

You'll do it? Good for you! Oh, Socrates!
Come out! I've brought this son of mine to you,
though he's reluctant.

Socrates

           This one's still a baby!
How could he learn the ropes in a place like this?

Pheidippides

You learn the ropes: go off and hang yourself! 870

Strepsiades

God damn you, boy! How dare you curse your teacher?

Socrates

You hear how he said 'wopes'? How babyishly,
with his wittle wet wips all slack and pouty?

---

[1]When the Spartans invaded Attica in 445 Pericles was said to have bribed
their King, Pleistoanax, to withdraw and to have used this phrase when
accounting for that expenditure of public funds.

And he's supposed to learn courtroom defense
and summonsing and how to bullshit juries?   875
But still, Hyperbolus learned—for a hundred grand.[1]

Strepsiades
Money's no object; teach him, he's a natural.
Why, when he was just a little tyke this high,
he could build sand-castles, carve a little boat,
he'd put together cars from balsawood   880
and frogs from lemonpeels, as pretty as you please!
Just see that he learns that pair of Arguments,
the Better, whatever that is, and the Worse,
the one that makes the weaker case the stronger.
Or, if not both, at the very least the Worse.   885

Socrates
He'll learn all that from the Arguments themselves;
I've other things to do.[2]

Strepsiades
                    But just remember:
he's got to learn how all just claims are countered!

SCENE IX

(Better Argument, Worse Argument, Chorus Leader)

Better Argument
Come on out here, be a star,
exhibitionist that you are!   890

Worse Argument
At your service: the bigger the crowd,
the faster I shall have you cowed.

Better Argument
Cow me? Who do you think you are?

Worse Argument
An Argument.

Better Argument
                    But inferior!

---

[1]The only place in comedy where Socrates is portrayed as a teacher of a
politician, as he was accused at his trial of having been the teacher of
political figures who had harmed the democracy.

[2]The actor who plays Socrates must now play one of the Arguments. A choral
song would be structurally normal after line 888 and would have allowed
the actor time to change his costume, but Aristophanes apparently stopped
work on his revision of the play before he had written one.

Worse Argument
  I'll refute you anyway.

Better Argument
  What could you possibly do or say?   895

Worse Argument
  Deploy some fancy principles.

Better Argument
  They're all the rage with these imbeciles![1]

Worse Argument
  Geniuses!

Better Argument
            I'll lay you flat!

Worse Argument
  Tell me how you'll accomplish *that*.

Better Argument
  By speaking what is just and fair.   900

Worse Argument
  And I'll refute it with hot air!
  I say that Justice doesn't exist.

Better Argument
  Oh no?

Worse Argument
            Then tell me where she is.

Better Argument
  Among the gods does Justice dwell.

Worse Argument
  Zeus locked his father in a cell   905
  with impunity: how so, pray tell?[2]

Better Argument
  Yuk! This is getting worse and worse;
  give me a basin, I'm nauseous!

Worse Argument
  Sprung a leak, you poor old fart?

Better Argument
  Shameless faggot, little tart!

---

[1]Pointing to the audience.

[2]After overthrowing his father Cronus and the Titans, Zeus imprisoned them
  in the underworld: behavior contrary to the Greek principle of honoring
  one's parents.

Worse Argument
Thank you!

Better Argument
You're a clown to boot!   910

Worse Argument
What compliments!

Better Argument
A parricide too!

Worse Argument
Don't you know those names are gold?

Better Argument
They were lead in days of old.

Worse Argument
Nowadays they bring you credit.

Better Argument
You're a swine!

Worse Argument
And you're decrepit!   915

Better Argument
You've made the younger generation
uninterested in education.
Just wait until the Athenians
find out what fools you've made of them!

Worse Argument
You're moldy.

Better Argument
While you're well-to do.   920
But recently you were destitute,
claiming to be a king in rags,
with brilliant thoughts in a paper bag.[1]

Worse Argument
How clever—

---

[1]Literally, 'claiming to be Mysian Telephus and munching the ideas of Pandeletus out of a little bag'. Telephus, King of Mysia in the mythical Trojan War period, was the subject of a play by Euripides (produced in 438) who disguised himself as a pitiful beggar in order to plead his cause; *Telephus* is extensively parodied in Aristophanes's *Acharnians* of 425. Pandeletus was a popular politician and prosecutor of the 430's; his connection with the character Telephus is unclear but would make sense if Pandeletus' eloquence and (pretentious?) ambition seemed at odds with his relative lack of wealth or family distinction.

Better Argument
> How bizarre—

Worse Argument
> your allusions!

Better Argument
> that you are   925
> supported by our nation while
> its tender youth you quite defile!

Worse Argument
> This boy you'll never teach, old fool.

Better Argument
> I will, to keep him safe from you
> and your blabbering ineptitude.   930

Worse Argument
> Let him rave; come here, my lad!

Better Argument
> Touch him and I'll crack your head!

Chorus Leader
> Stop your fighting and abuse!
> *You* expound just how you used
> to educate the men of old;   935
> *you*, the modern teacher's goal.
> After judging the pros and cons,
> the boy will choose the school he wants.

Better Argument
> Fine by me.

Worse Argument
> And fine by me.

Chorus Leader
> OK, so who will take the lead?   940

Worse Argument
> He can have it;[1] whatever his line,
> I'll shoot him down with phrases fine,
> concepts novel and thought sublime.
> Result? If he so much as sighs,
> I'll sting his face and both his eyes   945

---

[1]Worse Argument is so confident as to be indifferent to the order of speaking in the contest; but he is probably aware that the last word tends to be the most effective. In all of Aristophanes's formal debates (except the one in *Wealth*), the first speaker ultimately loses.

with intellectualities
as fatal as a swarm of bees!

AGON[1]

*(Chorus, Chorus Leader, Better Argument, Worse Argument, Strepsiades,
Pheidippides)*

Chorus (5[1])

Now's your opportunity	
to show superiority	
in intellectuality	950
and verbal ingenuity.	
Everything is now at stake	
for higher education's sake;	955
for those in our dear coalition[2]	
this is the crucial competition.	

Chorus Leader

You who crowned the men of old	
with solid traits of character,	
lift your voice in joyful speech	
and tell us what your nature is.	960

Better Argument

Very well: I'll now describe	
what education used to be,	
back when I spoke truth and flourished,	
back when decency was in vogue.	
First of all, a boy was expected	
not to make the smallest noise.	
Boys would march along the streets	
to school at the music master's house,	
orderly squadrons of them, almost	
naked, even in the snow.	965

---

[1]The *Agon*, or formal debate, is a standard structural feature of Old Comedy consisting of formal arguments in long-verses by two contestants, each argument prefaced by a choral song and a two-line introduction by the chorus leader; the chorus leader usually presides and may (along with the idle contestant) interject comments or questions to break up or otherwise enliven the long speeches. In this *Agon*, as in the *Agons* of *Knights* and *Frogs*, the arguments are differentiated rhythmically: the Better Argument speaks in anapests, the Worse in iambics (a less dignified rhythm).

[2]Ambiguous: the spectators will suppose that the Clouds' friends are Socrates and his cohort, but in fact the Clouds will end by punishing the Socratics. Even during this *Agon* the Clouds speak sympathetically to Better Argument but not to his opponent.

Then he'd have them memorize
    a song—and keep their legs apart!—
'Pallas Dire City-Sacker',
    or 'What a Cry Sounds From Afar',
tuning their voices to the mode
    their fathers handed down to us.
Any of them played the clown
    by jazzing up the melodies—   969[1]
all the rage today, that awful
    dittybopping Phrynis[2] played—
that one got a good old-fashioned
    thrashing for ruining the tune.
When in gym class, all the boys
    would cross their legs when sitting down,
so they'd not expose to the grownups
    anything provocative.
When they rose again, they'd have to
    smooth the sand they'd sat upon,   975
careful not to leave behind
    the marks of their manhood for lovers to see.
No boy then would dare anoint
    himself below the belly-button:
thus their genitals were dewy
    and downy, like a succulent peach.
Nor would he liquify his voice to
    simper softly to his lover,
prancing around with goo-goo eyes
    as if he were pimping for himself.   980
Nor when dining could he reach for
    even a single radish-head,
no, nor grab for celery
    or dill from any grownup's plate,
no hors d'oeuvres, no canapés,
    no crossing legs at dinnertime!

---

[1]The standard line-numbering includes an anonymously attested line (970) that is in the proper meter and concerns musical styles but was not transmitted as part of the play; it was inserted by the seventeenth-century scholar L.C. Valckenaer but is not considered genuine by modern editors.

[2]Phrynis of Mantineia was a famous cithara player credited with introducing the sort of rhythmical modulations complained of here; his victory in the Panathenaic musical competition in 456 probably contributed to the adoption of this new style by Athenian players.

Worse Argument
    Antiquated rubbish, full of
        crickets[1] and prehistoric rites,
    moldy tunes and sacred oxen![2]

Better Argument
    Isn't that precisely how   985
    my generation's education
        bred the men of Marathon?[3]
    You, by contrast, teach our boys
        to swaddle up in cloaks from birth,
    such a turn-off when they're dancing
        at Athena's festival,[4]
    one of them with his shield held low,
        afraid he'll get his hambone poked!
    Thus, my boy, be bold and opt for
        me, the Better Argument.   990
    You shall learn to loathe the market,
        to shun the public baths as well,[5]
    to feel ashamed of what is shameful,
        to burn with rage at any slight,
    to offer your seat to any grownup
        you may see approaching you;
    never to treat your parents rudely,
        never to act disgracefully
    or any way that might dishonor
        the sacred shrine of Modesty;   995

---

[1]Before the Persian invasions, which ended in 479, well-to-do Athenians had worn golden crickets as brooches in their hair.

[2]Referring to the Dipolieia, an ancient agrarian festival for Zeus that featured the elaborate ritual sacrifice of an ox.

[3]In 490 an expeditionary force under the Persian King Darius landed at the bay of Marathon and marched toward Athens (26 miles SW). At the town of Marathon they were met and defeated by an Athenian-Plataean army. This victory, considered by Athenians to be their most glorious, ended Darius' European ambitions, and the Persians did not invade again for ten years, when they returned under Xerxes. Later legend told how one Pheidippides (or Philippides) ran back to Athens to report the good news. Although he reportedly dropped dead of fatigue as soon as he had done so, the marathon race still commemorates his run.

[4]The Panathenaia, held in July, was the principal festival for Athena and (along with the theatrical festivals for Dionysus) the most lavish of the year. One of the events was a martial dance performed by warriors naked except for a shield.

[5]Places frequently mentioned as hang-outs for young men.

never to invade a go-go
    dancer's house and lose your head,
making the whore get sweet on you,
    thus shattering your good repute;
never to contradict your father,
    calling him Methuselah,
laughing at how old he is,
    forgetting how he reared you!

Worse Argument

Follow *this* advice, my boy,
    I swear by Dionysus   1000
people will call you Casper Milquetoast,
    just like the sons of Hippocrates.[1]

Better Argument

No, you'll spend your time in gyms,
    your body hale and glistening,
not chattering in the market about some
    thorny topic, like modern boys,
not getting dragged to court to settle a
    disputatious nuisance case.
No, down to the Academy[2] you shall go,
    and under the sacred olive-trees   1005
crown yourself with reeds and race
    with fine upstanding boys your age,
redolent of briar and leisure
    and the catkins flung by the poplar trees,
glorying in Spring's return,
    when plane trees whisper to the elms.

Follow up on my suggestions,
give them serious consideration,   1010
then you'll be in proud possession
of a chest that ripples, skin that gleams,
shoulders humongous, tongue petite,
buttocks of iron, prick discreet
But follow the path of modern boys   1015
and *this* is the look you'll soon enjoy:
shoulders narrow, pasty skin,

---

[1]Hippocrates, a nephew of Pericles, had three sons frequently ridiculed in comedy for having misshapen heads (a family trait) and for being boorish and ill educated.

[2]Academeia was a park sacred to the local god Academus, with a stream, wooded paths and sporting fields; later Plato chose it as the site of his school.

sunken chest, tongue gigantic,
buttocks tiny, prick titanic,
motions long winded.[1] Listen to *him*,
you'll think what's bad is good, 1020
what's good is bad. Moreover,
you'll catch a serious disease:
Antimachus' faggotry![2]

Chorus (5^2)

What masterful proficiency
in wisdom fair and towering, 1025
each word with virtue flowering!
Happy the men of old indeed!
You who must reply to *that*,
you with your clever line of chat, 1030
must now find something new to say;
your opponent has spoken splendidly.

Chorus Leader

It seems you'll need some awesome schemes
    to bring to bear against him,
if you hope to overtake the man
    and not become a big joke. 1035

Worse Argument

My guts have actually been churning
    quite a while now, longing
to demolish everything he said
    with considered refutations.
I got the name Worse Argument
    among the intellectuals
for just this very reason, that
    I pioneered a new technique,
a logical way to contradict
    established laws and morals. 1040
And *there's* a skill that guarantees
    a million dollar income:
to take the cases that are worse
    but nevertheless to win them.
Observe the way I cross-examine
    his vaunted pedagogy.
Now, first of all, he won't allow
    hot water in your bathtub.

---

[1]Punning on 'motions' presented to a political assembly.
[2]Known only from comic references to his effeminacy.

So tell me, please, the principle
   on which you scorn hot water.   1045

Better Argument
   Because they're utterly base and make
      a warrior a pussy.

Worse Argument
   OK now, wait! I've got you in
      a hammerlock already.
   Just tell me, which of Zeus' sons
      you think the greatest he-man,
   the one you think most spirited
      and performed the greatest labors?

Better Argument
   I judge no man superior
      to Heracles the mighty!   1050

Worse Argument
   In that case, have you ever seen
      a Heraclean cold bath?[1]
   And yet, who was manlier than he?

Better Argument
   That's just the sort of quibble
   the teenaged boys spend all their time
      expatiating over,
   that makes the bath-house popular
      and leaves the gym deserted!

Worse Argument
   And loitering in the market-place
      you forbid, while I commend it.   1055
   If the market's such a sleazy place,
      then why did Homer always
   call Nestor 'man of the *agora*',
      and every other wise man?[2]
   And now the question of the tongue,
      which my opponent flatly
   forbids young men to exercise,
      while I would strongly urge it.

---

[1]Natural hot springs were known as Heraclean because they were popularly
thought to have been created by Athena or other friendly gods for Heracles
to bathe in during the course of his wanderings and labors.

[2]A sophistic argument: in classical Athens the market place (*agora*) was the
commercial 'downtown' area of the city, while in the Homeric epic poems
agora meant 'gathering place for deliberation'.

He also insists on modesty;
     another bad idea.   1060
For where has anybody ever
     seen a man get famous
and rich by being modest? Well?
     Just name him, and I'm refuted.

Better Argument
     A lot of people. Peleus got
     his knife for being modest.[1]

Worse Argument
     A knife you say? A charming piece
          of profit! Lucky devil!
     Hyperbolus, who manufactures
          lamps, has made a million   1065
     through sheer dishonesty, but never
          got a knife, I'll grant you![2]

Better Argument
     And Peleus got to marry Thetis
     for being very modest.[3]

Worse Argument
     And then she up and left him flat
          because he wasn't man enough
     to satisfy her in the sack
          when the lights went off at nighttime.[4]
     For women like their loving rough;
          but you're an ancient ruin.   1070
     Just look, young man, at all the toil
          the virtuous life consists of,
     and look at all the fun you stand
          to lose, if you pursue it:
     young boys, young women, games of chance,
          good eating, drink and laughter.

---

[1]Achilles' father Peleus, during a visit to the hero Acastus' house, refused the amorous advances of Acastus' wife, who then accused him of attempted rape. Acastus had Peleus taken unarmed to the forest to be eaten by wild animals, but the gods pitied him for his honorable character and gave him a knife to defend himself.

[2]For Hyperbolus see 552 n.

[3]Since the sea nymph Thetis was destined to bear a son mightier than his father, the male gods arranged to have her married off to a mortal man.

[4]As in all folktales involving mermaids and mortals, Thetis returned to the sea; the standard story was that Peleus had annoyed her by interrupting a magical ceremony by which she was making Achilles immortal.

Why live a life at all if you're
    deprived of all these pleasures?
OK, then, let's proceed to look
    at the necessities of nature.[1]   1075
Let's say you've messed up, fallen in love,
    been taken in adultery.
You're screwed if you can't talk your way
    out of trouble. Come with *me*, though,
you'll indulge your instincts, leap and laugh,
    consider nothing shameful.
If taken in adultery
    you'll tell the angry husband
there's nothing wrong with what you did,
    that Zeus himself's the culprit: 1080
for even Zeus falls victim to
    a lust for lovely women,[2]
so how can you, a mortal man,
    be stronger than the sky-god?

Better Argument

But say he gets his anus reamed,
    and his whatsis baked with ashes?[3]
What kind of argument would he use
    to keep his asshole narrow?

Worse Argument

What harm is there in turning out
    to have a gaping asshole?[4]   1085

---

[1]Contemporary philosophers drew a sharp distinction between customs and laws (which they saw as social inventions) on the one hand, and nature (which they thought of as a universal imperative) on the other, a distinction that amoralists could use to justify conduct that law or custom would prohibit.

[2]Zeus was indeed one of the great philanderers of mythology; in Euripides' play *Trojan Women*, Helen uses the same argument to justify her adultery with Paris of Troy. The often unethical behavior of the gods in myth had become an embarassment for traditional moral philosophers, some of whom denied the truth of such myths.

[3]Under Attic law a cuckolded husband could do what he liked with an adulterer, including killing him or exacting a monetary compensation. The husband might also make a public example of an offender by pushing a radish into his anus, singeing his genitals with hot ashes and plucking out his pubic hair.

[4]The conventional way of referring to a male who had submitted himself to anal penetration by another male and had thus reduced himself to the condition of women, slaves and prostitutes. For citizen males such behavior was not merely a disgrace but a crime punishable by debarment from the

Better Argument
You mean, what greater harm could be
endured than a gaping asshole?

Worse Argument
And what would you say if I refute
your argument on this point?

Better Argument
I'll close up shop; what else could I do?

Worse Argument
All right, then, here's a question:
What type of person is a lawyer?

Better Argument
A gaping asshole.

Worse Argument
                    Quite correct.   1090
And what about a tragic poet?

Better Argument
Gaping asshole.

Worse Argument
                    Right you are.
And what about a politician?

Better Argument
Gaping asshole.

Worse Argument
                    Now you see,
your argument was total crap!   1095
What about the audience there,
the majority?

Better Argument
                    I see them now.

Worse Argument
And what do you see?

Better Argument
                    The majority,
by god, are gaping assholes! Him,
at any rate, and that one there,

---

exercise of civic rights. Nevertheless, comic poets routinely assumed that
political advancement entailed prostitution, much as humorists today as-
sume that women with celebrity or power must have offered sex to attain
it.

and that one with the longish hair!   1100

Worse Argument
So, what do you have to say for yourself?

Better Argument
I'm beaten! Here, you dirty fags,
for heaven's sake please take my rags,
I'm deserting to your side![1]

Worse Argument
What now? You want to take this son of yours   1105
away, or have me teach him oratory?

Strepsiades
Why, teach him and discipline him, and don't forget
to put sharp edges on his tongue. One edge
for hacking little lawsuits; hone the other
for cutting into meatier affairs.   1110

Worse Argument
Don't worry, he'll come home a seasoned sophist.

Pheidippides
More likely, I think, a wretched pasty-face.

SECOND PARABASIS[2]

(Chorus, Chorus Leader)

Chorus
Go right ahead. But I imagine
that you'll come to regret this course of action.

Chorus Leader
Now we'll tell the audience the
goodies the judges stand to get,   1115
if they do this chorus a favor,
as by rights they ought to do.[3]

---

[1]Evidently Better Argument now wants to learn the secrets of oratorical success for himself and so dashes into Socrates' school (where he will change back into the role of Socrates).

[2]The ancient commentator Heliodorus noted that five verses from the first version of the play do not appear in their proper place between lines 1114 and 1115; probably Aristophanes removed them in the course of his revision. That this second parabasis has only a rudimentary choral introduction and only one *epirrheme* may be an indication of incomplete revision.

[3]The judges are the ten men whose names had been drawn by lot from a list of eligible men submitted by each tribe (there were ten tribes) and who swore to give an impartial verdict in voting on the relative merit of the

First of all, if you want to sow and
    plough your fields when the season's right,
we will rain on your fields first, on
    others' only after you.
Then we'll act as guardians for
    all your crops and all your vines,
making sure they're never harmed
    by drought or by a drenching rain.   1120
Any mortal man who would
    dishonor our divinity,
let him learn from us the evil
    consequences he will face.
From his farmland he will take no
    wine or any other crop;
when his olive trees and vineyards
    start to bloom with tender shoots,
just as quick we'll shoot them off with
    bullets from a stormy sky.   1125
Let him try to dry his bricks, we'll
    make it rain torrentially,
then we'll blast the tiles off his
    roof with hailstones big and round.
When he's getting married himself,
    or any friend or relative,
all night long we'll make it rain,[1] and
    thus he'll start to wish he were
a resident of Egypt rather
    than a man who miscast his vote.   1130

SCENE X

(Strepsiades, Socrates, Pheidippides)

Strepsiades
Twenty-sixth, twenty-seventh, twenty-eighth, then twenty-ninth,
and after that the day of days, the day
that makes me tremble, shudder and shit my pants,

---

competing plays. Each judge wrote down his ranking on a tablet and put it
into an urn; the presiding official (the *archon*) drew five of the tablets at
random to determine the order of prizes. The sort of appeal to the judges
that our chorus makes was not uncommon in Old Comedy.

[1] A main event of an Athenian wedding was the evening, torch-lit procession
of family, friends and guests that escorted the bride to her new home; hard
rain would not only ruin the procession but would also be taken as a bad
omen.

because the very next day's the Old and New,[1]
and every single creditor I owe   1135
has sworn to sue me, ruin me and destroy me.
I've made some fair and reasonable requests—
'Look here, my man, this payment isn't urgent;
please put this off, forgive that'—but they refuse
to deal on any such terms. They call me names,   1140
like chiseler, and promise to drag me into court.
Well, let them drag me now! I couldn't care less,
if Pheidippides has learned his lessons well.
I'll soon find out, if I knock at the Thinkery.
Boy! Boy, I say! Boy!

Socrates
                              Hello, Strepsiades!   1145

Strepsiades
Hello. But first, a little gift from me;
one's got to butter up the teacher some.
And tell me, has my son been able to learn
that Argument you recently brought on stage?

Socrates
He has.

Strepsiades
                    Omnipotent Trickery, that's great!   1150

Socrates
So you can beat whatever rap you please.

Strepsiades
Even if witnesses saw me borrow the dough?

Socrates
Even if thousands of witnesses saw you do it.

Strepsiades[2]
Then I'll shout a fortissimo shout!
Creditors, eat your hearts right out!   1155
And eat your principal and interest too!
No longer am I scared of you!
What a son I'm having reared
within this edifice right here,

---

[1]The last day of the month, when lawsuits could be lodged, was thought to
have a double identity because it stood between the outgoing and the
incoming month.

[2]Elements of the following song by Strepsiades and of the lyric dialogue
following it parody contemporary tragic (especially Euripidean) style.

with a gleaming switchblade for a tongue,   1160
my fortress, my estate's salvation,
my enemies' enemy! Surely he
will rescue his dad from calamity!
Now run inside and summon him here to me.
My child, my boy, come forth from out these halls,   1165
to thy father lend an ear!

Socrates
Here is the man thou seekest.

Strepsiades
Dear, dear boy!

Socrates
Claim him and depart.

Strepsiades
Hurrah, hurrah, my child! Wow,   1170
how great it is to see your pale complexion!
You're obviously ready to take the fifth,
to rebut accusers. You've sprouted that true Athenian
expression, the Who-Me? look of being wronged
when you're guilty, even of serious crimes. I know   1175
that look, and I see it blooming on your face!
So save me, since it was you that ruined me.

Pheidippides
And what are you scared of?

Strepsiades
                                    The day that's Old and New.

Pheidippides
You mean there's a day that's old and also new?

Strepsiades
The day my creditors plan to sue me, yes!   1180

Pheidippides
They'll lose their cases, then. There's just no way
a single day can possibly be two days.

Strepsiades
It can't?

Pheidippides
            How *could* it be? Unless you also
maintain that a crone can be a girl as well.

Strepsiades
But that's our custom, anyway.

Pheidippides

I think the law 1185

is improperly understood.

Strepsiades

So what's the point?

Pheidippides

Our venerable Solon was a natural democrat.[1]

Strepsiades

I've yet to see the connection with Old and New Day.

Pheidippides

Well, Solon established the summons for two days,

for the Old Day first and then for the New Day second, 1190

so that sureties would be scheduled for the new moon.

Strepsiades

What purpose did the Old Day serve?

Pheidippides

Dear sir,

it allowed defendants to come a day in advance

to settle their cases if they chose; and if they didn't,

they'd have a serious problem on new moon day. 1195

Strepsiades

Then why don't magistrates accept the sureties

on new moon day, but only on Old and New Day?

Pheidippides

They're like the officials in charge of sacrifice:

they want the cash deposits a day in advance

to get an early start embezzling tidbits. 1200

Strepsiades

All right! You pitiful fools who sit out there,

you're money in the bank for intellectuals,

you're rock-heads, sheep, a bunch of empty jars!

I've got to sing a song for me and my son,

a jubilant paeon to our joint success! 1205

Strepsiades, happy happy man,

whom no one else is smarter than,

---

[1]Solon, who held the archonship in 594/3, was credited with inventing the traditional Athenian law code. Although he could hardly have been a democrat (it took democracy another century to establish itself at Athens), fifth-century Athenians tended to believe that the man to whom they credited the laws should also be credited with their form of government.

who also raised his son to be
a paragon of mentality!
My friends and neighbors will agree,
with envy they will all turn green,   1210
when this son of mine has speechified
and got my lawsuits nullified!
But now, my son, let's take a break,
and have a feast to celebrate.

SCENE XI

(Strepsiades, First Creditor with Witness, Second Creditor)

First Creditor

Am I supposed to kiss my money goodbye?
I won't! I shouldn't have made the loan at all,   1215
a brazen refusal instead of all this hassle.
And now I'm dragging *you* along to serve
as witness to my foolish loan. What's more,
I'm sure to make an enemy of my neighbor.
But I'd rather die than be unpatriotic![1]   1220
I hereby serve Strepsiades—

Strepsiades

                    Who's there?

First Creditor

—to appear on Old and New Day.

Strepsiades

                    Audience, note
that he's summoned me for different days. What charge?

First Creditor

The twelve thousand that I lent you for the purchase
of the charcoal-colored horse.

Strepsiades

                    Horse? Listen to that!   1225
Why, everybody knows I can't stand horses!

First Creditor

By Zeus, you swore by the gods you'd pay me back.

Strepsiades

By Zeus, when I swore that oath Pheidippides
had yet to learn the unshakeable Argument.

---

[1]To equate bringing a lawsuit with patriotism is a joke on Athenian litigious-
ness.

First Creditor
And that's your reason to deny the debt?   1230

Strepsiades
I'm entitled to *something* for educating him.

First Creditor
You're ready to swear by the gods you owe no debt,
wherever I specify?

Strepsiades
What sort of gods?

First Creditor
Why, Zeus, Poseidon, Hermes.

Strepsiades
Certainly Zeus;
I'd even pay a buck to swear by him!   1235

First Creditor
Then shame on you, and may you roast in hell!

Strepsiades
That belly of yours would make a real nice wineskin.

First Creditor
Oh! Mock me, will you?

Strepsiades
It'd hold five gallons.

First Creditor
Almighty Zeus and all the gods, you won't
get away with this!

Strepsiades
The gods! How funny!   1240
To swear by Zeus is a joke among the learned.

First Creditor
In time you'll get your just deserts for this!
For now, just tell me plainly whether or not
you'll repay your debt.

Strepsiades
Hold on a sec, OK?
I'll come right back with an answer to your question.   1245

First Creditor
What do *you* think he'll do? You think he'll pay?

Strepsiades
Now where's the guy that wants my money? Sir,

do you know what this is?

First Creditor
>   That? Why, sure. A thermos.

Strepsiades
And *you* want money, being such a fool?
I wouldn't trust you with a single dime,   1250
for saying thermos when you should say thermé[1]

First Creditor
I take it you won't pay.

Strepsiades
>   That's *all* you'll take.
Now take a hike, and make it snappy too;
get out of here.

First Creditor
>   With pleasure. But rest assured,
I'm filing suit, if it's the very last thing I do.   1255

Strepsiades
You lost twelve grand; why lose a lawsuit too?
I wouldn't want you to have to suffer that,
merely because you foolishly said 'a thermos'.

Second Creditor
Oh woe is me!

Strepsiades
What's that?
Who's making lamentation here? It couldn't   1260
be one of Carcinus' gods who made that sound?[2]

Second Creditor
Why seekest thou to know who I may be?
Let 'man accursed' suffice.

Strepsiades
>   Then take a hike.

Second Creditor
O deity cruel, o mischance that unhorsed
my chariot-rail! Athena, my undoing!   1265

---

[1]See 669 ff.

[2]Carcinus was a tragic poet; presumably a lamenting god had figured in one or more of his plays. Lines 1264-65 are lines that had been spoken by Alcmene in the tragedy *Licymnius* by Carcinus' son Xenocles.

Strepsiades
And what's your beef against Tlepolemus?[1]

Second Creditor
Don't mock me, sir, but tell that son of yours
to pay me back the money that he borrowed,
if only in sympathy for my bad luck.

Strepsiades
What money is that?

Second Creditor
                                    The money that he borrowed.   1270

Strepsiades
You're really badly off, it seems to me.

Second Creditor
God yes! While charioteering I lost my grip.

Strepsiades
The way you're raving I'd say you lost your mind.

Second Creditor
Me rave? Is it raving to want my money back?

Strepsiades
A hopeless case of lunacy.

Second Creditor
                                    How so?   1275

Strepsiades
In my opinion, your brain's completely scrambled.

Second Creditor
In *my* opinion, you're gonna get sued, by Hermes,
unless I get my money.

Strepsiades
                                    So tell me this:
do you think that when Zeus makes it rain, the water
is always different, or do you think the sun   1280
draws up from below the very same water again?

Second Creditor
I haven't got a clue, nor do I care.

Strepsiades
Then how can you demand your money back,
if you're ignorant of meteorology?

---

[1]In Xenocles' tragedy (see the previous note) Alcmene's half-brother had been
killed by her grandson Tlepolemus.

Second Creditor

    All right, if you're short of money, pay at least   1285
    the interest.

Strepsiades

              Interest? Please define that term.

Second Creditor

    You know: the property borrowed money has
    of growing larger and larger, daily and monthly,
    as the stream of time flows on?

Strepsiades

                      That's very well put.
    Now then, the sea: would you say it's larger now   1290
    than it used to be?

Second Creditor

              God, no; it's just the same.
    It's unnatural for the sea to grow.

Strepsiades

              Then how,
    you wretched fool, though rivers flow to the sea
    but the sea does not grow larger, do *you* attempt
    to make *your* sum of money grow in size?   1295
    So prosecute yourself right off my property!
    Boy, fetch my stick!

Second Creditor

             I'm taking note of this!

Strepsiades

    Get going! Giddyup, you gelded nag!

Second Creditor

    Atrocious assault!

Strepsiades

           Move out! You want a whipping?
    You want me to jam this up your thoroughbred ass?   1300
    Just look at him run! I knew I'd get you moving,
    for all your chariot wheels and teams of steeds.

Chorus

Chorus (6[1])

    How dangerous to entertain
      a lust for villainy,
    like *this* old man, who'd now evade   1305
      the debts he ought to pay.
    Before the day has run its course

the time will surely come
when our old sophist feels remorse
about the harm he's done. 1310
I think that he will soon obtain
the answer to his prayer:
a son who's able to maintain
what's unjust and unfair. 1315
And though the son wins every case
with wickedness and lies,
perhaps, *perhaps* his dad will pray
his tongue gets paralyzed. 1320

SCENE XII

(Strepsiades, Pheidippides)

Strepsiades
Help! Help!
Oh neighbors, kinsmen, fellow villagers!
I need your help right now, I'm being beaten!
Oh Lord! My unlucky head! My face! My jaw!
You scum! You'd beat your father?

Pheidippides
                    That's right, dad. 1325

Strepsiades
You see? He admits he beat me!

Pheidippides
                    Sure I do.

Strepsiades
You scum! You parricide! You criminal!

Pheidippides
Please call me all those names, and add some more.
You know, I enjoy it when you call me names?

Strepsiades
You giant asshole!

Pheidippides
                    Flatter me some more! 1330

Strepsiades
You'd beat your father?

Pheidippides
                    Yes, by God; what's more,
I'll prove it's right to do so.

Strepsiades
>What a scumbag!

Just how could it be right to beat a father?

Pheidippides
I'll show you with unbeatable arguments.

Strepsiades
You could beat me in an argument like *that*?

Pheidippides
>Quite easily.   1335

Just choose which argument you plan to use.

Strepsiades
Which argument?

Pheidippides
>The better or the worse.[1]

Strepsiades
I guess you've learned your lessons well, my boy,
to argue against what's just, if you can make
this case convincing, that it's just and right   1340
for fathers to be beaten by their sons.

Pheidippides
But all the same I think I can convince you,
and you'll have nary a point to make against me.

Strepsiades
And I can't wait to hear what *you* will say.

SECOND AGON

(Chorus, Chorus Leader, Strepsiades, Pheidippides)

Chorus (7[1])
Your job, old man, is to conceive   1345
>how you'll refute this lad;

for had he nothing up his sleeve
>he wouldn't act so bad.

Yes, something makes him confident
in being boldly insolent.   1350

Chorus Leader
How this fight originally
>began, the Chorus wants to know.

---

[1]Pheidippides is not only ready to defend an outrageous proposition but does not care whether it is true or not, being prepared to argue either side.

Tell us what the motive causes
    were; you'll tell us anyway.[1]

Strepsiades
Certainly I'll tell you why we
    first began to scream and shout.
You'll recall I held a feast to
    celebrate my son's success.
First I asked him quite politely,
    Grab your lyre and sing that song,   1355
'Ram Got Shorn and Who's Surprised?',
    the song by old Simonides.[2]
He replied that playing the lyre is
    absolutely out of date,
so is singing at a banquet,
    like a grandma husking corn!

Pheidippides
You're the one who ought to have been
    stomped and beaten then and there,
asking me to sing a song, as
    if you're entertaining crickets!   1360

Strepsiades
That's the kind of thing he said the
    whole time we were partying.
And on top of that he called
    Simonides a total hack!
Nonetheless I held my tongue, as
    aggravated as I was.
Then I asked if he at least would
    put a garland on his head,
read me something by Aeschylus;[3]

---

[1] Aristophanes pokes fun at the structural convention of Old Comic *Agons* that required the Chorus to introduce each speaker in the debate; see the note on the first *Agon* (above, 947 ff.).

[2] Simonides of Ceos was an internationally celebrated poet of an older generation (his dates are *c.* 556-468); this song was a victory ode for a wrestler who had defeated one Crius (whose name means 'ram') at the Nemean Games in the late sixth century.

[3] Aeschylus was the greatest tragic poet of the era that saw the Greek victory over the Persians and the establishment of the Athenian empire (his dates are 525-456), so that men Strepsiades' age tended to regard him as the embodiment of the ethical values that had made such achievements possible. In Aristophanes' play *Frogs* (produced in 405), Aeschylus is pitted against Euripides (whom Aristophanes regarded as embodying the inferior values of his own era) in a contest of poetic and moral power.

he right away replied (I quote), 1365
'I regard old Aeschylus as
    being first among our bards:
first at incoherence, noise and
    words as steep as mountaintops'!
You can just imagine how I
    almost had a heart-attack!
Still, I held my temper, bit my
    tongue and said, OK, my boy,
read me something clever by a
    modern poet, if you can. 1370
Right away he tosses off some
    discourse by Euripides,
how a brother—holy moly!—used to
    screw his own sister!![1]
That was it; I'd stand no more, and
    started to abuse the boy,
using lots of bad and shameful
    words. As you can guess,
he began to match me word for
    word, and then he jumps right up, 1375
bashes me and punches me and
    chokes me, totally trashes me!

Pheidippides
Had it coming, anyone who
    doesn't praise Euripides,
cleverest of poets.

Strepsiades
                Clever?
Him? You—what's the word I want?
Better not say, get punched again.

Pheidippides
That's right, and you'd deserve it too!

Strepsiades
How deserve it? I'm the one who
    raised you! Do you have no shame? 1380
I'm the one who understood your
    baby-talk and what it meant.

---

[1]Euripides (see previous note) was fond of treating provocative myths in provocative ways; the allusion here is probably to the incestuous relationship of Aeolus' children Macareus and Canace and their concealment of the resulting child, which Euripides dramatized in his play, *Aeolus.*

You said 'dwik' and I would know to
   go get something for you to drink.
You demanded 'bob' and I would
   fly away to bring you bread.
Then before you'd even finish
   saying 'poopie' I'd be there,
taking you to the yard to do it.
   Just now, though, when you began   1385
strangling me, and I yelled and shouted,
   I'm about to shit! you balked,
   wouldn't take me to the yard—
   villain!—but you strangled on,
   made me do a poop right there!   1390

Chorus (7^2)

   The young men's blood is up to know
      their counterpart's reply:
   should he be glib enough to show
      that what he did was right,

   there's nothing that could make me choose   1395
   to be in any father's shoes!

Chorus Leader

   Now's your chance, you word-mechanic,
      shooter of the latest rap:
   find a way to talk us into
      thinking what you did was right.

Pheidippides

   What a joy to hang around with
      everything that's new and hip,
   being free to disregard all
      customary laws and norms!   1400
   Just a while ago, when all I
      wanted was the cavalry,
   I could barely speak three words
      before I stumbled over them;
   now, since dear old dad here made me
      put a stop to all of that,
   I'm at home with subtle thoughts, with
      words and contemplations,
   confident that I can show you
      why it's right to beat my pa.   1405

Strepsiades

   Back to the cavalry, then, dear God! It's

> better for me to spend my dough
> keeping up a team of horses than
> > serving as your punching-bag!

Pheidippides

> Let's return to my earlier point, the
> > one you made me interrupt;
> answer me this, to start things off:
> > did *you* beat *me* when I was small?

Strepsiades

> Sure I did; I cared for you, and
> > did it for *your* own good.

Pheidippides

> > > > Then look: 1410
> isn't it just as right for *me* to
> > care for *you* in a similar way,
> inasmuch as one's own good
> > depends on being beaten up?
> How's it fair that your own body
> > stays immune but mine does not?
> After all is said and done, I'm
> > a free-born man, the same as you.
> 'The children scream; you think the father shouldn't?'[1]   1415
> You'll reply it's customary
> > that only children suffer this;
> I reply with a well-known fact:
> > old age is a second childhood.
> What is more, it makes more sense for
> > older men to scream than younger:
> they're the ones with less excuse to
> > stray from good behavior.

Strepsiades

> Nowhere does the law permit a
> > father to be so treated.   1420

Pheidippides

> Wasn't it a man who wrote the
> > law originally, a man
> just like you or me? And didn't

---

[1]Adapting a line (691) from Euripides' play *Alcestis* (produced in 438), in which Admetus, who seeks a volunteer to die in his stead, has rebuked his own father Pheres for refusing to do so, and Pheres replies, 'You like the daylight; you think your father doesn't?'

he persuade the men of old?[1]
Why should I not have the right
  to argue for a different law,
valid for tomorrow's sons, that
  henceforth they should beat their dads?
All the beatings that we took
  before the new law took effect   1425
we forgive our fathers, we
  declare an amnesty on those.
Take a look at poultry now, and
  all such other animals:
don't they stand up to their fathers?
  Aren't we animals, more or less,
save that animals don't propose
  decrees the way we humans do?

Strepsiades
Well then, if you want to ape the
  animals in everything,   1430
why not also eat your dung and
  sleep on wooden perches too?

Pheidippides
Not the same, dear fellow, nor would
  Socrates accept that line.

Strepsiades
Then I say, stop beating me, or
  someday you'll regret you did.

Pheidippides
Why is that?

Strepsiades
          As things now stand, I
have the right to punish you;
you will have the right to punish
  your son.

Pheidippides
         If I have a son.   1435
If I don't, I've screamed in vain, and
  you'll be laughing in your grave!

---

[1] The historicist version of social-contract theory, which considers laws to have
been invented at particular times by particular people in order to create
civilization out of anarchy, is first attested in the late fifth century in the
writings of the oligarch Critias, one of Socrates' most notorious pupils.

Strepsiades
Age-mates in the audience, I
    think that what he says is right:
give the younger generation
    credit for making a valid point.
There's no reason why they shouldn't
    beat us if we don't behave.

Pheidippides
I've got one more point to make.

Strepsiades
No, it'll be the death of me!   1440

Pheidippides
Not at all. You might be less
    annoyed about your suffering.

Strepsiades
How is that? Explain how you can
    benefit me in all of this.

Pheidippides
Beating mother as I beat you!

Strepsiades
What's that? What did you say just now?
That's a different and far worse matter!

Pheidippides
What if, with Worse Argument,
I could justify to you   1445
mother-beating as a law?

Strepsiades
My response is, if you do,
I don't give a damn if you
end up being put to death,
right along with Socrates   1450
and Worse Argument as well!

SCENE XIII

(Strepsiades, Chorus Leader, Pheidippides, Pupils, Socrates)

Strepsiades
You Clouds, it's all your fault I suffer this!
I trusted you to handle my affairs.

Chorus Leader
No, you're responsible for doing it to yourself:
you took the twisting road that leads toward evil.   1455

Strepsiades
Why didn't you tell me that at the very start,
instead of leading a poor old clod astray?

Chorus Leader
We do the same thing every time we see
a man who's fallen in love with what is wrong;
we cast him down in sheer calamity   1460
until he learns devotion to the gods.

Strepsiades
Alas, O Clouds, a lesson hard but fair!
I shouldn't have tried to cheat my creditors
of their money. Now, my dearest boy, what say
that bastard Chaerephon[1] and Socrates   1465
we go and murder for cheating us this way?

Pheidippides
I couldn't lift a finger against my teachers!

Strepsiades
'Yea verily respect Paternal Zeus!'[2]

Pheidippides
Paternal Zeus! Just listen! How old-fashioned!
Does Zeus exist?

Strepsiades
                He does.

Pheidippides
                        He doesn't either,   1470
'cause Vertigo deposed him and now reigns.

Strepsiades
He hasn't really. I thought he had, myself,
because of that object over there. Poor sap,
to think I took some pottery for a god!

Pheidippides
Well, rant and rave to yourself; I'm going in.[3]   1475

Strepsiades
What lunacy! Damn, I must have been insane,
to drop the gods because of Socrates!

---

[1]See line 104.

[2]A quotation from an unknown tragedy.

[3]Probably 'in' to his own house, since it is unlikely that Strepsiades would set
the Thinkery on fire if his son were inside.

Well, Hermes old boy,[1] don't be annoyed with me
or bring me some disaster, but pity me
for acting crazy because of their idle talk.   1480
You be my lawyer: should I slap them with a suit
and prosecute them? I'll do as you advise.[2]
That's good advice! I shouldn't cook up lawsuits,
but rather, quick as I can, burn down the house
of these con-men. Xanthias, come here! Xanthias!   1485
Go get the ladder and a hatchet, too,
then climb up on the roof of the Thinkery
and break the tiles—do it for your master!—
until the house caves in on top of them!
And someone else go get me a lighted torch.   1490
Today they're going to pay for what they've done,
and I don't care how fast they run their mouths![3]

Pupil 1
Help! Help!

Strepsiades
All right, my torch, throw up a lot of flame!

Pupil 1
Hey, what are you doing, man?

Strepsiades
                   What do you think?   1495
I'm engaged in subtle argument with your house!

Pupil 2
Oh no! Who's making a bonfire of the house?

Strepsiades
Remember me? The guy, you stole his coat?

Pupil 2
You'll kill us, kill us all!

Strepsiades
                That's my intention!

---

[1]A small statue of the god Hermes, protector of wayfarers and patron of
businessmen (and thieves), stood on the street outside many an Athenian
house.

[2]Strepsiades puts his ear to the statue and hears (or feigns to hear) the god's
permission to attack the Thinkery.

[3]Strepsiades' vengeance may have called to mind an incident that had hap-
pened a generation earlier in the Italian city of Croton, where a Pythagorean
school of philosophy was set afire during one of its meetings and only two
of the philosophers escaped alive.

I only pray the hatchet does its job   1500
before I fall somehow and break my neck!

Socrates
You! You on the roof! The hell you think you're doing?

Strepsiades
I walk aloft and contemplate the sun!

Socrates
I'm done for! Help! I'm going to choke to death!

Pupil 2
I'm done for too! I'm going to burn to death!   1510

Strepsiades
Then what were you up to, laughing at the gods
and peering at the backside of the moon?
Pursue them,[1] hit them, stone them for many crimes,
but most of all for injustice toward the gods!

Chorus Leader
Lead the dancers on their way;   1515
we've done our dancing for today.

---

[1]An apparent stage-direction indicating that the inhabitants of the Thinkery
flee instead of being burned alive.